The Pheno
Through

and
Resources to Optimize Wellness

By

Dr. Sebastian Caliendo
DC, MS, LAc, DipLAc, DACBN

"Paying it Forward"

I am excited to announce that 100% of the profits from this book will be donated to the Tunnel to Towers Foundation. Over 90% of all donations directly provide mortgage-free homes for first responders and war vets who have sacrificed life and limb for their country. In addition, Tunnel to Towers also pays off existing mortgages for these heroes.

www.PhenomenonOfHealing.com

Disclaimer

Please be advised that the material in this work is provided solely for information and should not be interpreted as medical advice or instruction. No action or inaction, for that matter, should be taken solely on the contents of this publication. Instead, the reader should consult with their doctor on any matter relating to their health and well-being. The information and opinions are believed to be accurate and sound, based on the best judgement available to the author. However, readers who fail to consult with appropriate health professionals assume the risk of any injuries. The Food & Drug Administration has not approved the material in this book. The information discussed in this book is not intended to diagnose, treat, cure, or prevent any disease. Thank you for your consideration in this matter.

Table of Contents

Foreword, Introduction

Part One: Healing Observations and Determinants

Part Two: Suggestions for a Healthy Lifestyle

Dedication

This work is dedicated to my Ilka, "Bella," the love of my life; my beloved departed parents, Fanny and Sasty, who showed through their example how to be the first to love; all my family and friends who encouraged me to attempt this improbable endeavor; the mentors who blessed my life and taught me to have more of a compassion to serve rather than a compulsion to survive; and finally to all of you who dare to *Be all that you can be.*

Acknowledgments

This book would not have been possible without the support and encouragement from my family and friends, as well as some colleagues.

First and foremost, I would like to express my sincerest gratitude to my special lady Ilka Lipetz for her unconditional love, which inspires me every day. Thank you for all of your help, especially in picking out the book cover, showing this dinosaur how to save files on the computer, taking photos for my website, and some of the graphic designs for Facebook.

Special thanks to:
Dr. David Minkoff and Glenn Poveromo for writing the forewords to my book.
Dr. David Friedman for his professional literary advice.
My colleague and good friend, Dr. Frank Reinhardt, for his computer skills editing some of the book's lay out.
My Daughter Victoria Lyn for her encouragement and inspirational support and for using her creative talent to help design the web page.
My grandson Alex Caliendo for helping with editing and the self-publishing through Amazon.
Kellie Berry for her beautiful graphic design work (which she did pro bono).
Beth Racine for working with me on the developmental editing.
Erik Mathre for designing the web page.
My longtime friend and colleague Jeanne Denaro for her editorial insights.
Faith Benesh, Bill & Joan Barrett, and Jon Reynolds for taking photos for the website.
Mrs. J Reed for allowing me to use her beautiful painting for the front cover of my book.
Jon Reynolds for his help in developmental editing.

There have been many other people along my journey, who have encouraged me as well, so I apologize that it is not possible to list everyone, but I appreciate every one of you who have been supportive and a part of this experience in any way - you know who you are – thank you.

Foreword: Dr. David Minkoff, MD

Executive Director and Medical Director of LifeWorks Wellness Center in Florida, which treats patients from all over the world and is well known and respected in the field of integrative medicine. Author of The Search For The Perfect Protein.

Only a few years ago, Dr. Caliendo came into my office for an evaluation of his health. His bright smile and demeaner hooked me from his first "hello." Sometimes as a physician you meet a kindred spirit. That was my impression when I met Dr. C.

If you have ever met the good doctor, you know he has an infectious optimism about life and people and laughter. Though he came to me as a patient, we became immediate friends. We shared a viewpoint that life is a gift and that we have a duty to make the most of it.

Not only did we have doctoring in common, but also, he is an athlete of some magnitude as an amazing softball pitcher who can wheelhouse a pitch faster than a cheetah can run.

When I was five years old, I decided I wanted to be a doctor. I wanted to help. In my first 20 years, I did what every modern graduate does – I followed the teachings of the traditional school, pretended I knew what I was doing, and read journals looking for answers that did not seem to have many.

Too many times, what I did, did not work, and too many times my conscience kept me up at night telling me that I could be doing better.

But what? How?

In the end, these questions and doubts brought me to Biological Medicine – the idea that through working with natural law, better medicine could be practiced. For the last 23 years, that is what I have done. In 1997, my wife and I started a little clinic of integrative medicine that has now grown to be one of the largest in the US. We see patients from all over the world who come to get help with severe chronic illness. And most of them go home well.

What I practice is the medicine and attitude that is exemplified in this book you hold in your hands. It captures the truth of how the human body and spirit work and how to best help in its recovery.

Dr. C's book represents what the true spirit of medicine and healing and caring should be. If a doctor is a good one, half of their healing is through the love that they grant to their patients. This book is about that. Yes, diet and exercise are part of it, but the spirit alone can heal, and the troubled spirit causes a troubled body. The doctor who does not know that is out of touch. The patient who doesn't know that will have a slow recovery – or none at all.

We are spiritual beings, and we have bodies. Both must be nurtured for health to occur. In this book, you will find a guide for the path that can help you navigate both. Thank you, Dr. C, for a job well done.

Foreword: Glenn Poveromo

Transformational Coach and Author of *Change your Thinking, Change Your Life*

I have harbored a strong intuition regarding medical practitioners for as long as I can remember. A deep feeling in my gut always seemed to alert me as to who was a true healer and who was not. Although I was only mildly aware of this sensation as a young boy, still, it was a knowing that my subconscious mind kept stored in its memory. As I matured, the awareness of true healers began to fuel my conscious thoughts, and thus my journey of searching for healers began in earnest.

I have encountered a number of very special practitioners as I continued my quest; some were centered upon the practice of conventional Western medicine, while some were dedicated to alternative medicine, and some were a combination of both. Regardless of their delivery systems, a true healer simply offers healing. It was during the early stages of my journey that I became acquainted with, and was treated by, Dr. Sebastian Caliendo.

Dr. Caliendo was my softball teammate when we first met almost 40 years ago. I was drawn to his energy and was fascinated by his knowledge of the body and, even more, by all that he knew about the power and influence of our minds, hearts, emotions, and spirits in the healing process. These concepts were new and foreign to me at that point of the journey; however, my portal to higher understanding was opened through our conversations. I then became a patient of Dr. Caliendo's and witnessed his ability to facilitate healing on a firsthand basis.

I am uncertain that Dr. Caliendo knew that he has been the greatest singular influence of placing my feet upon the path toward learning all that I could in order to awaken my own ability to help others heal. As a result of his influence, I have become a Transformational Coach, and by following Dr. Calando's lead, I place my focus upon alerting my clients of the power of their mind, body, heart, emotion, and spirit to help them attain a state of peace and well-being.

I have written: "Simple Thoughts About Life & Living / Five Hundred Insights For Inner Strength And Happiness," as well as, "Change Your Thinking / Change Your Life / Learn To Live Your Best Life Possible," and, "Messages From Spirit," all of which have their origin in the wisdom and knowledge that Dr. Caliendo imparted to me many, many years ago.

The Phenomenon of Healing Through Intentional Love offers a wealth of information for those who are seeking to live their best lives possible. Dr. Caliendo has utilized expertise gathered through 45 years of offering health and healing to his patients. He has created a treasure trove of information that encompasses not only valuable insights regarding our bodies but includes with great clarity the integration of our minds, hearts, emotions, and spirits in this INCREDIBLE work of art. Through a favorite mantra, "There is no such thing as an incurable disease, only incurable people," Dr. Caliendo offers the reader a variety of healing techniques and modalities. He masterfully includes anecdotal accounts of patients for which he has been an instrument of healing, through his present time consciousness, pure intentions and God- given talent, as well as citing discoveries made by experts in the field of mind, body, and spirit. I highly recommend Dr. Caliendo's book to anyone seeking to maximize their journey of life.

Author's Foreword

I would like to make you aware of a poem I wrote 40 years ago concerning healing to commemorate the opening of Naturalife Wholistic Health Services that I established in 1979 (please note the name changed shortly afterwards to Naturalife Wholistic Health Center). Over the years I have given it to a handful of professionals in the healing arts whom I felt embodied the concepts put forth in this poem. Hopefully, after you have read it, it will "whet your appetite" to continue reading this work.

For quite some time many colleagues and friends have been asking me to write a book on my life's experiences where health is concerned. I never really took them seriously, for I had no clue how to accomplish such a feat. But here I am, after 45 years of clinical practice and eight years of retirement, attempting the improbable.

A Zen proverb says, "A wise man learns from his mistakes, but an even wiser man learns from others'." This concept surely applies when discussing the topic of health.

Hopefully, after you read this work, you will take advantage of my life's experiences where health is concerned. I have had a passion and interest in the healing arts since my formative years. Please let me explain. My early years can be described as those of a sickly child. In addition to contracting all the typical childhood diseases, I also had the dubious distinction of contracting Scarlet Fever (quarantined in a hospital for weeks), relapsed double lobar pneumonia, mononucleosis, and Melanoma, a very aggressive form of cancer. It was when I suffered a relapse of double pneumonia at age 13 that I read my first book on healing. I was quite ill, and not responding to traditional medical care. My parents were being treated by a chiropractor, Dr. Joseph Will, at the time, and he offered to make a house call to assess my condition. After examining me through palpation of my spine, he told my parents he was confident he could help me recover. He made several house calls over a couple of weeks to treat me with spinal manipulation with amazing results.

While I was recovering, he gave me a book to read on the history and philosophy of Chiropractic. After finishing this book, I knew this wonderful healing art was my calling. I immediately wrote to a Mr. Ralph Evans, who was then (in 1957) the Administrar of Palmer Chiropractic College in Davenport, Iowa, to learn more about their curriculum. He sent me the information I requested, and I was immediately sold on going there once I became of age. (I eventually did attend Palmer and graduated in 1966 as a Doctor of Chiropractic).

Over the years, I researched many healing modalities to increase my scope of practice. Many had merit, but some fell "short of the mark." In this work, I will only be discussing worthwhile information that can benefit the reader. Helping people was very gratifying yet frustrating when there were some patients I could not help. One of my professors at Palmer College told us that, regardless of how good a doctor you become, 80 percent of the patients you treat will get completely better, 10 percent will experience only slight relief, and 10 percent will not respond to care at all. Initially, I found what he had prophesied concerning patient outcome to be quite accurate in my practice. Well, this bothered me, thinking there must be *something* I could add to my armamentarium to help those who did not respond to my treatments.

As fate would have it, in 1969, I treated a patient whose daughter was blind in one eye due to a tumor pressing on her Optic nerve. I agreed to treat her with chiropractic care in conjunction with a famous Nutritionist, Dr. Henry Bieler, who put her on a specific dietary regimen which, after six weeks, in conjunction with intensive chiropractic care (approximately 15 treatments), restored the young girl's eyesight (this experience will be discussed in greater detail later on in this book). I was so impressed with this adjunctive nutritional care that I started attending nutritional seminars on weekends for several years while slowly introducing nutritional care into my "bag of tricks." I decided to go back to school for three more years in the mid-'70s to get my master's degree in biology, with an emphasis Nutrition from Bridgeport University and, in addition, eventually receiving my Diplomate status from the American Clinical Board of Nutrition. Without question, incorporating nutrition into my practice definitely enabled me to help more patients by increasing my scope of practice.

After witnessing the wonderful results, the acupuncturist at our Wellness Center achieved with patients who did not respond to my care, I semi-retired in the mid-'90s to study acupuncture. I attended The New Center for Wholistic Health Education and Research for three years, attaining my acupuncture degree, and eventually received my Diplomate status from The National Certification Commission for Acupuncture and Oriental Medicine.

This amazing healing art markedly increased my scope of practice even further from a holistic perspective. In the final analysis, treating patients from a holistic perspective was very gratifying, especially having the opportunity to successfully treat difficult cases referred by my colleagues.

Having a thirst for more knowledge, I continued attending pertinent health-related seminars during my years in practice. I mention all this not to impress you with my accomplishments but to emphasize the great range of options available in the field of alternative health, which I want to share with you to improve your quality of life. In the latter part of this work, I will share some self-help tips that I found to have great merit.

The Wholistic Healer

Someone who has the compassion to serve,
Rather than just a drive to survive.
Faith in his science, philosophy and art,
Willing is he to give from his heart.

Someone who cares and is truly concerned,
Not merely into how much that is earned.
Someone who radiates within and above,
Striving for oneness with God, who is love.

Someone who practices whatever he preaches,
Thus, giving strength to whoever he teaches.

Someone creative and truly with vision,
Striving, achieving his lifetime ambition.
Eager to serve his sisters and brothers,
Knowing that joy comes from doing for others.

Someone who truly masters his art,
Graciously speaking – straight from the heart.
Someone whose intent is simple and pure,
Knowing that it is not he that can cure.

A true healer shares many skills from his store,
Growing and learning to heal more and more."

~ **Dr. Sebastian Caliendo,**
DC, LAc, DipLAc, DACBN

It has also been said that there is nothing new under the sun. I mention this to bring attention to the fact that much of the information shared in this work should be considered common knowledge. It is information I have gleaned from close to 50 years of attending literally over 100 health-oriented wellness seminars and reading countless books and articles on this subject that I considered essential for a healthy lifestyle. Granted, there may be other worthwhile measures that can be beneficial to achieve a healthier lifestyle. However, the recommendations shared in this work are measures I employed while practicing and in my private life with very favorable results. Therefore, as I initially mentioned, a wise person learns from another person's experiences, so I believe it would behoove readers to take advantage of my life experiences where health information is concerned. Indeed, I tried remedies over the years that never achieved the promising beneficial health benefits claimed, which, for obvious reasons, I will not mention. Understand, I have done all the "in vivo" research for you, and I am sharing what I know will be of health benefit to my readers. A Chinese saying etched in glass in the atrium of my Health Center, written by the famous Chinese sage Lao Tzu, said, "The journey of a thousand miles must begin with the first step." Hopefully, for those of you new to this concept of taking responsibility for your health, this work will be the first step on your journey to a healthier and happier life.

Carpe Diem!

Note: The beautiful illustration on the front cover of this book, titled "Come unto Me," which displays the hands of God, was painted by Joann Reed in 1967. A copy of this portrait was gifted to me in the early '70s by John C., a patient I treated and who responded favorably to my care through the grace of God. Fortunately, I never gave it away since I believe it serves as a perfect invitation to peruse this work. Thank you, Mrs. Reed, for allowing me permission to use your beautiful painting for the book cover. Both you and your husband, Don (whose hands you used to model the painting), are very special believers in God's Love.

Like most of us, I have experienced some "bumps in the road" along the way on life's journey. Fortunately, they were more of an exception rather than the rule. Many blessings have been bestowed upon me during my life through the grace of God. Therefore, as a token of my gratitude, I would like to "pay it forward" by donating any proceeds from the sale of this work to one of my favorite charities, "Tunnel to Towers." The mission of the Stephen Siller Tunnel to Towers charity is to honor the sacrifice of firefighter Stephen Siller, who laid down his life to save others on September 11, 2001. This charity also honors our military and first responders who continue to make the supreme sacrifice of life and limb for our country. At the time of this writing, this charity has built over 1,000 mortgage-free smart homes for our military and first responders in need, and possibly facing homelessness, with the monies raised from this charity. In addition, monies are also applied to pay off existing mortgages for these heroes. Unlike many other charities, where CEOs receive large salaries from donations, Stephen's brother, Frank Siller, takes no money to run this program.

Mission Statement

The initial intent for creating this work was to leave a legacy for my friends and family. The fact that this is supposed to be the first generation expected to have a shorter life span than their parents disturbed me. Therefore, I decided to create a treasure trove of resources and information from my life experiences where health is concerned. I hoped that, if applied, it could help them avoid being a part of that statistic. In addition, I wanted them to realize why anything less than a loving thought could be harmful to their health and why they should always strive to be the first to love. However, considering the times we live in now, I truly believe this book is "just what the doctor ordered" for its contemporary social significance. Its concepts can be applied to anyone seeking to live a more peaceful, happier, and consequently, healthier life, reminding us that, like the song says, "All You Need Is Love." Blessings!

"Make your journey worthwhile by having the compassion to serve rather than the compulsion to survive."

~ Dr. Sebastian Caliendo

Introduction

There have been many good, informative books written with a real penetrating insight concerning the workings and complexities of the human body. However, in this particular work, I will focus on my interpretation of how the body actually heals, through the Grace of God, from the perspective of one's state of consciousness and Quantum Physics. To achieve this, I feel it is my duty first to help build your confidence and understanding of the body's ability to heal itself and to help you realize that, with the exception of congenital abnormalities, "There is no such thing as an incurable disease, only incurable people" (a quote coined by the compassionate oncologist and author, Bernie Siegel). I will employ scientific evidence concerning the body, along with case histories, testimonials, analogies, parables, and fables, to accomplish this goal.

Part Two contains a discussion of how the body functions from a holistic perspective, emphasizing the basic tenets of holism. The first is teaching people how to take responsibility for their health by offering resources to optimize their health. The second is to help readers understand that to achieve total health, one has to treat the whole person and not just the condition itself in isolation.
As a side note, western medicine's approach to healing is quite different. While it has made great strides toward advancing health in this country, especially in the area of trauma and emergency care, it falls short of the mark when addressing chronic health challenges.

Unfortunately, in this age of specialties and sub-specialties, western medicine, for the most part, only treats the symptoms and not the cause of the health imbalance, which requires treating the whole person from a holistic perspective. This approach is like shutting off the fire alarm in a burning building while failing to address the fire which triggered the alarm.

Not to mention, in many cases, treating the symptoms and not the cause of a health condition with drugs can cause some harmful side effects after being prescribed for an extended period. While I appreciate the merits of western medicine, I believe the future in health care should focus on an integrative approach to health care which is slowly becoming more accepted as a viable approach. This system combines practices and treatments from alternative medicine and conventional western medicine. In an ideal world, one should employ natural alternative medicine first, integrative medicine second, and lastly, even surgery when indicated.

I believe the ideal medical setting would have a Lifestyle coach as an adjunctive service in a doctor's office since many chronic conditions can be traced back to an unhealthy lifestyle. In this scenario, if indicated, the patient's symptoms can be treated for a short time with medicine until their symptoms abate, while at the same time having a Lifestyle coach address the possible cause of their condition.

That is, after a thorough assessment, necessary changes can be suggested to improve their poor lifestyle habits. God willing, this concept will become a reality someday.

Listen, we have often heard the phrase "Life is a gift," but many of us fail to realize that it is the state of one's health our body provides that enables us to enjoy this gift from God. Hopefully, you will embrace some, if not all, of these concepts to improve not only the quality but the quantity of life after reading this work. God bless.

Part One:
Healing Observations and Determinants

Chapter One

My Story

In the late summer of 2006, I visited one of my daughters (I have four daughters and one son) in Pennsylvania, where she stayed at the time. Fortunately, due to the sweltering weather, I was wearing a tank top. Why was that fortunate, you might ask? Let me explain. My daughter, Victoria Lyn, a licensed aesthetician, noticed a mole on the back of my left arm that she said looked very suspicious. She showed it to me with a mirror, and I realized it was abnormal due to its irregular shape and color (black). Due to its location on my arm, I never would have noticed it had my daughter not brought it to my attention. I made an appointment with a dermatologist when I returned home.

After examining the site, the doctor took a biopsy and sent it to a lab for a diagnosis. When the results came back, I was informed I had Melanoma, a very aggressive form of cancer that required surgery immediately. The surgery was performed in early October. My surgeon informed me that he removed all the cancerous tissue at my post-op visit, and no further intervention was needed.

However, after reading the biopsy report, I felt some concern, for it revealed the Melanoma was quite deep. Fortunately, shortly after my post-op visit, I attended a wellness symposium. One of the speakers spoke of a new blood test available in Greece that could detect cancer in a very early stage while the signs and symptoms were still sub-clinical (no apparent signs or symptoms).

This new test took one's blood and challenged it in a lab with agents to see if tumors would form. Fortunately, the little voice inside me told me I needed to take this groundbreaking test. It required me to have my blood drawn and then shipped in Dry Ice to Greece. Sure enough, after a couple of weeks, I received a 20-

page report confirming my suspicion.

The report stated my blood showed my cancer was still present but in early stage1A. The report was unique in that it made recommendations for treatment based on my biochemical individuality. In addition, the report gave optional treatment plans for either a traditional oncological approach recommending specific chemotherapy drugs for my biochemistry or an alternative protocol recommending specific supplements, IV drips of vitamin C, Ozone therapy, and injections of a specific form of mistletoe. The report also warned what supplementation was contra-indicated for my biochemistry.

Although I knew which protocol I would opt for, I decided to see an oncologist for his opinion on this cutting-edge report. The Oncologist I saw was a wonderful, caring man who mentioned having heard of this new blood test from Europe but never had a patient that had this test, nor had he ever had the opportunity to read this type of report. He told me quite candidly that he had never treated a patient in such an early stage of cancer (stage 1A). He said time was still on my side but cautioned that he needed to design a protocol soon due to the aggressive nature of Melanoma.

He said the dilemma was designing a not too powerful protocol that might compromise my immune system yet strong enough to eliminate the cancer. He then mentioned he wanted to confer with some of his colleagues to help design such a protocol. He felt that time was of the essence. He hoped to have a program designed in two weeks at the most, which he believed I should begin immediately, cautioning that waiting too long to decide would almost guarantee the Melanoma would become very advanced and treatment possibly having a poor outcome. Two weeks passed by, and, as promised, the oncologist called me at home one evening to discuss the protocol he and his colleagues had designed for treating my stage 1A Melanoma. He mentioned he would be "shooting from the hip" but believed that considering my unique situation he should give me chemotherapy for one month and follow up with

Interferon for one year. He said I would probably experience some flu-like symptoms while on this protocol for the year but said he could dispense some drugs to help with the symptoms.

I thanked him for "going the extra mile" to help me, then mentioned I decided to go the alternative care route. He told me I did not realize how aggressive this type of cancer could be and asked me to reconsider. I then asked at what point in time would it be too late to opt for his protocol if I was not responding favorably to alternative care. He thought waiting more than six months would result in a poor outcome, since this type of cancer was so aggressive. I thanked him for his effort and true concern for my health. I then assured him I would contact him within the six-month time frame if additional blood tests showed no improvement.

Following the recommendations for alternative care mentioned in the report, I eliminated all forms of sugar in my diet. It is gratifying to note that my blood test came back negative for cancer after being on this protocol for three months. It has now been over thirteen years that I am cancer-free, and I thank God daily for my new lease on life. It has been said that "adversity brings with it seeds of equal or better benefits." Going through this ordeal taught me not to take life for granted and to have an attitude of gratitude for all the blessings in my life.

Chapter Two

Mary's Story

During the late 1960s, when I was only in practice for a few years, an exciting event took place that would eventually change my perspective on healing. I was giving my normal lecture one evening on the benefits of chiropractic care to new patients. However, on this particular evening, a new patient named John approached me after the lecture to discuss his daughter and her rare medical condition.

He said he was intrigued by a statement I had made during the presentation claiming there was no such thing as an incurable disease, only incurable people (coined by the well-known author and oncologist Dr. Bernie Siegel.) He then explained that his daughter developed an inoperable tumor on her Optic nerve, which rendered her blind in her left eye.

Not willing to accept the fact that her condition was permanent, John began researching non-traditional alternatives. He eventually brought Mary to a Nutritionist, Dr. Henry Bieler, who was well known for the books he had written on Nutrition and successfully treated conditions nutritionally considered hopeless by traditional medicine. John was surprised I did not know who this doctor was since Bieler had written books on nutrition and was quite famous (understand, I did not know, nor did I have any interest at that time in the subject of nutrition). He then asked if I thought chiropractic care would be a valuable adjunct to this doctor's nutritional regime that Mary was following. I told John I would treat her under two conditions.

First, he would have to notify the doctor of his intent to have Mary receive regular chiropractic care in conjunction with his nutritional protocol. Second, I would treat Mary "pro bono," so there would be "no harm, no foul" if her sight did not return. He agreed, and to my surprise, the doctor also thought having chiropractic spinal manipulations would be a valuable adjunct to his nutritional protocol. One must realize this event took place over 50 years ago when chiropractic treatment received strong resistance from the American Medical Association. By the way, it is gratifying to note that there is a definite improvement in the rapport between both professions today, and chiropractic is slowly being recognized and accepted as a viable healing art by the general public.

By this time, I am sure you are wondering how Mary responded to the combined efforts of this nutritional doctor and myself employing both chiropractic and nutritional care simultaneously. Praise God! Wouldn't you know, after six weeks of intensive chiropractic spinal manipulation combined with Mary's individualized nutritional regime supervised by Dr. Bieler, the tumor was broken down by her body, relieving the pressure on her Optic nerve, and her eyesight was restored? When Mary returned to the hospital that made the initial diagnosis, she was reexamined, and tests showed the tumor was gone. When her father suggested it was the alternative care she received that was instrumental in her recovery, the doctor rejected that possibility. He said John could believe whatever he wanted. However, the condition resolved itself and should be considered a "spontaneous remission," for which there is no medical explanation.

Meanwhile, John was appreciative of the care I rendered to Mary. He presented me with one of the books written by the doctor I collaborated with when treating Mary, *Food Is Your Best Medicine,* by Henry G. Bieler. Needless to say, after seeing the results Mary achieved and reading this book on nutrition which John gifted me, I developed a burning desire to learn more about nutrition. I began reading books and articles and attending seminars related to nutrition, which I found fascinating. I eventually went back to college at Bridgeport University for three years, where I received my master's degree in Biology and Nutrition.

The more I learned, the more excited I became to share the information I learned about the fantastic ability of the body to heal itself.

Chapter Three

The Force is with You, but Are You Really Healthy?

When inquiring about a good and competent doctor for a health issue, you often hear a well-meaning person recommending a particular doctor because he/she "cured" them of their condition. Let me be clear: no doctor anywhere, including yours truly, has ever "cured" anybody of anything. Only the body heals — nothing else. A good doctor acts as a facilitator in the healing process and realizes that, in the final analysis, it is the body that does the curing. The most highly regarded doctors in their particular field, including surgeons, will usually state they have done everything humanly possible and now will have to wait to see how the body will respond to their care. The body utilizes its life force for healing to take place. Some call it "Innate Intelligence"; the Chinese refer to it as the "chi." But, regardless of what name you call it, not only is it impossible to heal without it, life as we know it would cease to exist without this wonderful phenomenon.

If you took a piece of meat and cut it down the middle, would it be able to heal if you wrapped it in a bandage after it was sewn back together or after giving it an antibiotic? You are probably saying to yourself, "What a silly question—it is a dead piece of meat!" Exactly. However, suppose we backtracked a couple of weeks when the animal was still alive, and the animal cut itself on a piece of barbed wire while grazing in the same part of its body. Would it heal? Probably, if the right measures were taken in a timely fashion to treat the laceration. So, what is the difference? Well, the animal was still alive and possessed its life force, which is absent in a dead piece of meat.

Understand, I am not trying to undermine your confidence in doctors, but rather build within you confidence and an understanding of the fantastic ability of the body to heal itself. So, yes, my friend, the *Force is with you* and will remain with you the rest of your life.

Hopefully, you are beginning to develop an appreciation for the body's ability to heal itself. Perhaps it might be wise to offer you additional insight into how well organized the body is in its ability to heal through the phenomenon of homeostasis (the ability of the body to maintain and control its internal environment despite disturbances from external forces) by explaining one of the many specialized integrated functions of the human brain. The following analogy will hopefully deepen your appreciation for this wonderful body of ours.

Brain Power by the Numbers

Did you know that scientists have calculated that your brain controls, separately and collectively, approximately 37.2 *trillion* cells that comprise the human body? Allow me to try to put into perspective the enormity of the numbers we are discussing here.

If a 1,000-dollar bill were deposited into an account with no interest every single day of the year for three years and is never touched, the amount of money amassed would be approximately one million dollars, with the stack of 1,000-dollar bills being about four inches in height. Now, let's assume the same 1,000-dollar bills continued to be deposited daily, not for three years, or even 300 years, but for 3,000 years. The amount of money amassed over that period would then be about one billion dollars, with the stack of 1,000-dollar bills now reaching a height of 333 feet. Realize, the number of cells quoted to you is in the trillions, not billions. Therefore, that same amount of money would have to be deposited daily for three million years to have amassed one trillion dollars, and, by the way, that stack of 1,000-dollar bills would be about 63 miles high (but remember, that amount of cells in the body is not 1 trillion, but 37.2 trillion—so do the math—you are talking about a stack 2,343.6 miles high.) Hopefully, this little analogy will help you grasp the enormity of the number of cells that comprise your body and just how phenomenal your brain is to have the ability to control the function of all these cells, both separately and collectively, as previously mentioned.

Are You Really "Healthy?"

What is health? When posing this question to my patients over the years, I would usually get a remark claiming, "Health is feeling good all the time." Well, actually, if we were to check a dictionary for the definition of health, it states, "Health is a state in the body when all the organs in the body are functioning normally." Nowhere in that statement does it mention how you feel. What I am trying to point out to you is that your health cannot be measured by how good you feel. In other words, just because you feel good does not necessarily mean you are in a good state of health. The absence of symptoms does not always mean the presence of health. Unfortunately, we live in a symptom-oriented society. Granted, in recent years, there has been more of a thrust towards preventative care, which is a good thing; however, most people only consult with a doctor when they are manifesting symptoms. Symptoms are the body's warning signs to indicate some kind of imbalance. They are the advanced stage of a condition. Now, there are some people who, unfortunately, never even experience these "warning signs," which can lead to a dangerous scenario. A perfect example is a person who, without warning, dies from a heart attack. While paying their respect at the funeral home, someone exclaims, "This came quite unexpectedly; John was never sick a day in his life." Evidently, John was very sick, but, perhaps from having a high tolerance for pain, he never had any complaints of not feeling well. Hopefully, by making you more aware of the fact that feeling good is not always a good indicator of your health, you will make it your business to consult your doctor for a wellness check-up at least bi-annually. Remember, "An ounce of prevention is worth a pound of cure." Things are not always as they appear to be, as the following story illustrates:

The Hermit

There was a man who, for the most part, rarely left his home. The only time he left the house was in the early evening before dusk to walk his pet. This pet was very strange looking, to say the least. You see, this pet had a very long snout, no tail, very short legs, and appeared to have some type of skin condition covering its entire body. However, this man, who only stood about five feet in height, loved this strange-looking pet, and the feeling was mutual. Being a very structured individual, he would take this strange-looking pet out for a walk every day, at exactly the same time every evening at dusk, following the same path for their daily exercise. The path they traveled took them through a park, and they would finish up by walking down a very narrow alleyway barely wide enough for them to walk side-by-side. Though it was very narrow, the man opted to walk through this alley because it was a "short cut," which enabled him to get home before dark.

Well, as fate would have it, this one particular evening, he traveled the same path, but just when he was about to exit from the narrow alley, a large hulk of a man appeared in front of him. This man was about seven feet tall and was at least four hundred pounds of solid muscle. Also, by his side was a very large hound almost the height of the little man. As you could imagine, their size made it impossible for the little man and his strange-looking pet to pass unless the large man and his hound would step aside by taking a few steps back to clear the passageway in this narrow alley. The little man then proceeded to cordially ask the large man if he would be kind enough to step aside, thus allowing him to exit the alley. Well, the large man refused to step aside and instructed the little man to turn around and go back from where he came. However, the little man persisted, explaining he had to get home before dark, insisting it would be much easier for the large man to retreat a couple of steps and allow him clear passage. The large man was adamant and warned the little man that he would unleash his hound to attack his strange-looking pet if he did not turn around and would not be responsible for what would happen to the little man's pet.

The little man held his ground and cautioned the large man that unleashing his hound would be a grave mistake. Well, the large man lost his patience and unleashed his hound. It immediately attacked the strange-looking pet. A cloud of dust ensued, with blood and tissue flying everywhere. Amazingly, when the dust settled, the large hound was shredded to bits. The large man stood there horrified, hardly believing his eyes, and exclaimed, "Oh, no! What do you call that thing"? The little man replied, as a matter of fact, "A sawed-off alligator." The moral of the story: things certainly are not always as they appear to be.

The same could be said about your health.

Chapter Four

Life Span v. Lifestyle

Scientists claim that human beings are capable of living up to 120 years. The Bible (Genesis 6:3) states, "His Days Shall be One Hundred and Twenty Years." We also know that different body cells are constantly being broken down and replaced at different rates by new healthy cells as needed. For example, red blood cells have a normal life span of approximately 120 days, while heart cells are replaced about every 90 days. You might wonder where all these replacement cells came from. They actually come from your daily diet. In other words, the food you consume today will become walking, talking flesh and blood tomorrow. Pretty amazing, wouldn't you say? I mean, show me a chemist who can synthesize a slice of pizza into living human tissue, a function that is accomplished by your body routinely each day. Thus, you can appreciate the importance of a balanced, healthy diet. It's like putting high-octane fuel in your car instead of a regular grade. While it costs more, the higher-grade gas enables the car engine to run more efficiently, consequently increasing its life span and requiring less repair, which in the long run saves money. The same can be said for your diet. Organic food costs more than "fast food," but it supplies your body with all the micronutrients needed to help your body function more efficiently and increase your life span. All of which results in fewer visits to the doctor and reduced medical bills.

I just mentioned that scientists and the Bible agree that human beings can live up to 120 years (and we know that they don't agree too often). Given that fact, don't you think that our Creator would make sure all the organs of the body also have the same life span? Obviously, the ability is there to do so. Listen, let's just use some common sense here. If you or I were building a robot, and we had the ability to install circuits that would last as long as the desired life span of the robot, wouldn't we do so? Of course, we would. Well, I don't think we are as intelligent as the One who created us, do you? Yet, every day you hear of people at the early age of 50 or 60 years of age, and in some cases even younger, on a waiting list for organ transplants, and more dialysis centers being built to meet the need for the increasing number of candidates requiring this procedure due to malfunctioning kidneys. If it has been established that our life span is, in fact, 120, it can be deduced that organs failing at the age of 40 or 50 are not a normal phenomenon. They should function normally for your entire life expectancy of 120 years. Your journey through life can be compared to a candle. Once a candle is lit, it continues to shine brightly until it runs out of wax. Once all the wax is used up, it flickers once or twice and goes out. With the exception of accidents, under normal life conditions, your body should continue to function normally for your entire life span, go to sleep one night at the tender age of 120 years and then meet your maker because your life has run its normal course. (I first heard this at a lecture I attended over 50 years ago, given by the late great professor of Chiropractic, humanitarian Dr. Reggie Gold. Over the years, I have included this analogy in my lectures ever since. I also must give credit to this iconic man for other analogies, stories, and parables shared in this work which I have gleaned from listening to him speak at lectures and his home in Spring Valley, New York.)

Why is it then that the average life span is well below its fullest potential? Why is it rare for a person to live to be even 100? Why will this be the first generation not expected to live as long as their parents did? The answer is a toxic lifestyle. The laws of nature are being violated, which cumulatively have negatively impacted one's life span. For example, the air we breathe in our industrialized countries is polluted with chemical wastes, putting a burden on the body's immune system, and consequently, compromising a person's health, ultimately reducing their life span.

Unfortunately, the same can be said about the water we drink and the food we eat. It is estimated that the average person is exposed to approximately 80,000 chemicals a year, all of which have a cumulative negative impact on one's longevity due to overburdening the body's detoxification pathways (this process of detoxifying the body will be explained in greater detail later on in this book). Another factor has more of a negative impact on the human life span than all the other factors combined; I refer to it as "Stinking Thinking." If you haven't figured out what I am referring to, it is STRESS. (In the following pages, you will see how stress has such a harmful impact on the body).

To put this into perspective, there are certain cultures throughout the world where the people traditionally live to be over 100 years of age. The Hunzakuts living in the Himalayas, the Georgians in Russia, and the Yamamuri Indians of Brazil are good examples of people possessing a longer life span, even though their bodies are no different from people living in industrialized societies with a much shorter life span. The only difference that can explain this phenomenon is their lifestyle. Their environment – the air, water, and diet – is more pristine, resulting in these cultures not being subjected to the toxins produced by more industrialized countries. And, even more importantly, they do not allow their emotions and egos to rule their lives. They lead a simple life and do not let the normal stresses of life give them distress (stress without distress).

Chapter Five

Stress ("Stinking Thinking")

I truly believe that stress is the main negative influence impacting the quality and length of one's life. How is it that stress can have such a deleterious effect on the body? Stress, if sustained, can cause significant harm to your health. In 1949, Dr. Hans Selye, an endocrinologist, was awarded the Nobel Prize for his manifesto on what he termed the "General Adaptative Syndrome." As explained by Dr. Selye, this syndrome comprises three stages of the stress response: The Alarm Stage, the Resistance Stage, and the Exhaustion Stage. It is noted that a person may or may not experience all of these three stages since much depends on the event that triggered the occurrence.

Let me explain:

The Alarm Stage

This phase can be precipitated by a primary event such as a motor vehicle accident or a secondary event such as an important meeting. Both cases trigger a sense of danger, which causes the autonomic nervous system to send an "SOS" signal to the brain, which in turn sends its signals to all parts of the body to decide whether to "fight or flight," giving a burst of energy to the limbs of the body to work faster. In this stage, one also experiences physical signs of tension: an increase in heart rate, an increase of sweating, and breathing which can lead to digestive problems and high blood pressure, accompanied by a fearful facial expression. This stage is basically a survival mechanism employed by the body—an adaptive response to one's environment. For example, when cave dwellers encountered a saber-toothed tiger in prehistoric times, their stress alarms would go off, and one of two things would take place. They would either stay and fight or else run for their lives. If they avoided being devoured and managed to escape safely back to their cave, they would sleep off the narrow escape due to sheer exhaustion, thus allowing their body to recuperate and return to normal homeostasis (rebalanced body). Because their stress was not sustained but instead was "shut off" by rest, there were no harmful effects on their bodies, and thus they avoided going into stage two and possibly stage three of the stress syndrome.

The Resistance Stage

In this stage, modern people, unlike our caveman friends, get no relief from the initial alarm stage, so the body continues to resist until becoming exhausted. This can cause a whole host of problems, including the inability to sleep, loss of memory, impatience, secretion of the stress hormone cortisol, which causes the body to store fats leading to weight gain known as "belly fat," behavioral patterns, worry and anxiety, and becoming predisposed to a compromised immune system.

The Exhaustion Stage

In this phase of stress, the person becomes physically drained of energy, depressed, and indifferent towards life experiences. Eventually, this leads to complications, causing conditions such as ulcers, diabetes, and heart disease caused by chemical imbalances due to sustained stress.

In her book, *I Can Do It,* author Louise Hay puts this phenomenon of stress in its proper perspective:

> *"I think that stress is a fearful reaction to life's constant changes. It's an excuse we often use for not taking responsibility for our feelings. If we can put the blame out there on someone or something, then we can play the innocent victim. Being the victim doesn't make us feel good, and it doesn't change the situation.*
>
> *Often, we stress ourselves out because we have our priorities mixed up. So many of us feel that money is the most important thing in our life. This is simply not true. There's something far more important and precious to us—without which we couldn't live. What is that? It's our*

"breath." Our breath is the most precious substance in our lives, yet we take it for granted that our next breath will be there when we exhale. If we didn't take another breath, we wouldn't last three minutes. Now, if the Power that created us has given us enough breath to last as long as we shall live, can't we have faith that everything else we need will also be supplied? When we trust life to take care of all our little problems, then stress just melts away".

As a wise sage once said, "Let go, and let God," and accept the fact that you cannot always be in control (actually, rarely). Believe and trust that God's timing is perfect, and yes," your stress will "melt away."

Chapter Six

Thoughts, Feelings, Emotions, Beliefs, and Chinese Medicine

Now that we elaborated on the phenomenon of the stress response, let's continue to talk about how this *stinking thinking,* in my opinion, has more of a negative impact on health than all the other stressors previously mentioned combined (toxic food, air, and water). Understand that negative thoughts give rise to negative feelings. It can be confusing to talk about feelings and emotions.

You see, your emotions can generate your feelings. For example, if you experience the emotion of love, you can be feeling happy, content, peaceful, secure, etc. Also, you can have feelings without even having an emotion or a thought. For example, if you walk down a lonely dark street at night, you may get a gut feeling to be alert. It is an automatic alarm reaction that you do not have to think or emote about.

Lastly, your feelings can generate your emotions. In her book, *Feelings Buried Alive Never Die,* Karol Truman offers a good explanation of the difference between feelings and emotions in a simple illustration: "If you became very angry at someone but held the anger inside, this is a FEELING. However, if you became angry and let yourself explode, either verbally or physically, the feeling of anger would then be manifesting itself as an EMOTION. In other words, the EMOTION is the outward expression or reaction of the feeling, or the EMOTION is the result of an intense feeling and a thought coming together." These experiences of thoughts and feelings have their origins in our belief system. This will be covered later.

When I went back to school in the '90s to study the concepts of Oriental medicine, one of my classes discussed how different emotions can impact specific organs of the body. Did you ever wonder about why you can get "red in the face" when angry, or why, when being suddenly frightened, people can wet their pants?

Why people who worry constantly are more prone to ulcers? After 60 years of marriage, what about a person who suddenly dies of a heart attack only a few days after the death of his/her spouse, despite having no history of heart disease? The cause of these phenomena is all one and the same...*our emotions*...which are a by-product of our thoughts.

Chinese medicine tells us that anger dominates (has direct influence over) the liver, causing it to contract and release stored blood. Since blood carries heat and is a basic physics law that heat rises, the blood rushes up to the face, causing a "red face." Fear, it is said, dominates the kidneys, causing them to react to this emotion uncontrollably by voiding the bladder, resulting in a pants-wetting mishap. Worry dominates the stomach/spleen axis, causing an increased release of digestive enzymes, predisposing a person to ulcers. And finally, sorrow dominates the heart, causing a reduced blood flow to the heart, resulting in a massive fatal heart attack. Perhaps now you can understand why it is so important to be careful what you think about since thoughts are the origin of our emotions and can positively or negatively impact your health. Essentially, anything less than a loving thought can be toxic to our health. So, practice forgiveness, and you will receive "the hundred-fold" return that Jesus spoke of in the Bible. After all, "to err is human, to forgive divine." (from "An Essay on Criticism," by Alexander Pope).

One of my patients' experiences illustrates perfectly the negative consequences of carrying around negative emotions that are never addressed or resolved. She was diagnosed with rheumatoid arthritis and mentioned her previous treatment by quite a few alternative health care professionals, using many modalities, with no satisfactory improvement of her condition. She obviously was trying to take responsibility for her health, doing everything on her part, from an anti-inflammatory diet and herbs to low-impact aqua exercise, but to no avail. After listening to her health history, I proceeded to ask this patient if there was anyone in her life with whom she may have issues that she was unable or unwilling to resolve. Without hesitation, she immediately expressed her hatred of her nephew. I noticed her face became quite flushed and clenching of her deformed rheumatic hands from the emotions generated from mentioning her nephew, which revealed the obvious negative feelings she had towards him. At that point, it became quite obvious that there was a direct connection between her health issue and her disdain for her nephew, which was not being addressed, and possibly preventing her from having any positive results from any mode of therapy she had engaged in. Once she explained why she had such hostile feelings towards him, I told her that while I could understand her initial reaction and negative feelings concerning this person, that it was critical for her to forgive him because it was literally "eating at her" and precipitating this pro-inflammatory response in her body. I explained that a person is a prisoner to anyone with whom they may have an issue. I then recommended that she seek a therapist to discuss this issue further and mentioned two books that I felt would be of help, *Radical Forgiveness* by Colin Tipping and *Feelings Buried Alive Never Die,* by Karol K. Truman.

Unfortunately, this story did not have a happy ending. She was in denial, said that my rationale for the main cause of her condition was absurd, and left my office, never to be heard from again.

Understand, my rationale for making the origin of her condition as being related to her emotions is based on the Traditional Chinese Medicine diagnosis. That is, overuse of a body part (in this case, her deformed hands) can lead to a stagnation of energy which, if sustained, can predispose the area to degeneration (rheumatoid arthritis in this case). The excessive clenching of her fists, which was apparent when she displayed the emotion of anger, qualifies as overuse of that body part. Hence the degeneration of her hands.

Hopefully, this story will give you pause and possibly make you realize that if you have issues with anyone, you have to resolve them for the sake of your health. I believe anything less than a loving thought may be toxic to your health.

I mentioned earlier that everything begins with a thought. Well, according to David Burns, Professor Emeritus at the Department of Behavioral Sciences at Stamford University School of Medicine in his book, *Feeling Good: The New Mood Therapy Revised and Updated*, in addition to confirming the concept that our thoughts create our feelings, he goes a step further explaining the origin of our thoughts. Professor Burns describes this phenomenon as "being derived from world events, whether they are positive or negative, that one is exposed to, that is interpreted as a series of thoughts that continually flow through one's mind, which is referred to as 'internal dialogue.' It is not these events, but one's interpretation of them by their thought process that creates the feelings."

Without getting too medical about different regions of the brain that control this process (mainly the limbic system), realize that, according to Professor Burns, all experiences must be processed through your brain and given a conscious meaning before you experience any emotional response. Again, as Burns stated, it is not the event that a person is subjected to but rather how each person reacts (their perception) to that event that affects their thought process and, consequently, their feeling or mood. Therefore, we can say that our imagination is the engine of our thoughts, which eventually create our reality (I am referring to habitual thoughts and beliefs, not "passing thoughts").

Now might be a good time to explain the difference between *thoughts* and *beliefs*. Judy Wright, the author of more than 20 books and hundreds of articles on family issues, states that "Beliefs are an acceptance of truth without any proof. It is one's value system usually obtained by earlier experiences. Beliefs are thoughts that you just keep thinking over and over again. They may be rational and based on fact. They can also be irrational and based on something your parents, their parents, and their parents, and parents believed. Thoughts are ideas, plans, reasoning power, and mindless chatter. Thoughts by themselves have no power until we incorporate action and make them part of our belief system, which, as I mentioned earlier, creates our reality, how we see the world, whether it be factual or not. It is said that a positive belief can lead to a positive outcome, which leads to a bigger positive belief and so on."

Did you ever hear the phrase "Whatever you believe or conceive you will achieve?" That pretty much says it all where beliefs and thoughts are concerned.

By now, I am sure you realize how much I love to tell stories to make a point. The following is a story about the power of a belief:

The Eagle Chick and The Young Man

A young man regularly went mountain climbing with his father. The young man finally believed he was experienced enough to climb by himself, so, one day, without saying anything to his father, he went mountain climbing by himself to prove to his father that he was finally his own man. Sure enough, he climbed the mountain without any significant incident. Understandably, he was very proud of himself. Being excited about his feat, he was anxious to share his accomplishment with his father, so he could finally be acknowledged as a man. However, he realized that his father might not believe him. He decided he should bring something down that could only be found on the top of the mountain. After perusing the area, he came upon an eagle's nest, which fulfilled that requirement. The eagle's nest had some eggs in it. He poached one to prove to his father that he really did climb to the top of the mountain. When he finally returned home and showed his father the eagle egg to prove his feat of climbing the mountain, his father, rather than congratulating him on his great accomplishment, chastised him for taking the eagle egg. He then instructed the young man to go back to the mountain and return the eagle egg to its nest. The young man obeyed his father and began the long journey back to the mountain. However, by the time he reached the base of the mountain, he was exhausted, which was understandable, considering all the hiking he already had done that day. He then looked around, and once again, he noticed another nest. Only this time, it was filled with chicken eggs. He immediately breathed a sigh of relief and proceeded to carefully mix the eagle egg in with all the chicken eggs and then returned home. Well, nature eventually took its course, and all the chicken eggs, as well as the eagle egg, finally hatched. Time went by, and all the chicks, including the "eagle chick," ritually performed all the activities of daily living for chickens. Now, one day, when the "eagle chick" was looking for worms as chickens often do, it noticed an eagle flying majestically high in the sky. The "eagle chick" turned to its mother and said it wanted to fly like that eagle. The mother explained that it was a chicken and chickens cannot fly. She then made him promise that he would not do anything foolish like trying to fly because it would cause serious injury to himself. Well, unfortunately, the "eagle chick" accepted his mother's words as gospel truth and never did try to fly, even though he possessed the ability to do so. So, you see, "WHATEVER YOU BELIEVE OR CONCEIVE YOU WILL ACHIEVE."

I realize I've been spending quite a bit on this topic of thoughts, emotions, and beliefs, but I do so to emphasize their importance to your health. Therefore, I want to share with you the important research of renowned cell biologist Dr. Bruce Lipton, a research scientist. He has dedicated his life to understanding human biology and behavior. In his book, *The Biology of Belief: Unleashing the Power of Consciousness, Matter & Miracles,* Dr. Lipton discusses the relationship between the mind and body, life, and consciousness, backing up these new concepts with solid research. For example, he performed a study where he took blood samples from individuals to ascertain their baseline immunoglobulins (immune system antibodies). He then had the group focus on a negative thought. When the immunoglobulins were rechecked, the blood level of these antibodies was considerably diminished, which, if sustained, would eventually compromise their immune system. He then instructed them to immediately focus once again, but this time on a positive thought. The results were nothing short of amazing. Not only did the blood levels of their antibodies increase, they actually surpassed their initial baseline levels. In this groundbreaking book, he also discusses the breakthrough field of epigenetics, promoting the concept that our belief system and thoughts can influence gene expression.

Also, author and entrepreneur Dr. Masaru Emoto claims that human consciousness affects the molecular structure of water. He backs up this concept with some very compelling pictures of water crystals before and after being subjected to human thoughts. One of his experiments involved gathering water from a swamp-like environment and taking pictures of the water crystals with a high-powered microscope, which revealed crystals with a blob-like appearance having no delineated geometric borders. He then took this same sample of water and placed it in a jar in the middle of a table, surrounding the water with a group of people in a circle holding hands. He then instructed the group to articulate aloud only positive affirmations about the water, stating, for example, how water was the basis for life and how life would not be sustained without its presence. Dr. Emoto once again took pictures with the high-powered microscope of the swampy, murky water. Amazingly, these same water crystals that previously had no delineated borders morphed into beautifully defined crystals, thus demonstrating the impact that vibrations of human consciousness can have on the water.

In addition, he also showed how negative vibrations could have the opposite reaction. Emoto subjected a beautiful water crystal with defined, delineated borders and subjected the crystal to the negative vibrations of heavy metal rock music. When the crystal was reexamined under a microscope for analysis, Emoto noticed the borders had broken down and given rise to a hideous unformed blob of matter.

Now, consider the human body is composed of over 60 percent water. Also, the brain and heart are composed of 73 percent water. After considering Dr. Emoto's research, perhaps we should start "connecting the dots" and accepting the concept of how the mind, via our belief system, thoughts, and emotions, can indeed impact our body, either positively or negatively.

Chapter Seven

Thoughts, Vibrations, States of Consciousness, and Visualization

Now would be a good time to elaborate on the actual connection between thoughts and vibrations and states of consciousness. Listen, if you took a basic science course in high school, you were taught that matter could neither be created nor destroyed but only changed from one form to another. For example, water can be changed from a liquid state to a gaseous state when heated to a boiling point of 212 degrees Fahrenheit and a solid state of ice when subjected to temperatures below 32 degrees F. However, it is now known that in addition to this law of physics, it is also a fact that all matter, whether organic or inorganic, has a vibrational frequency, including one's thoughts. Different objects may vibrate at different frequencies.

Before I go any further, I feel it incumbent upon me to assume your background in energy and vibrations is limited. Therefore, let me briefly explain some of the terminology to afford you a more penetrating insight and appreciation concerning this subject. I said all matter (whether a rock or a human being) is composed of vibrational frequencies. So, what are vibrations, and from where do they come? Electrical and magnetic energy form the atoms of matter, and it is the constant motion of these atoms which generates vibrations.

What is frequency? A frequency is the number of occurrences of a repeating event per unit of time. It is measured in Hertz and equal to one event per second. Frequencies manifest as wave vibrations. The top of the wave (known as the crest) is the pulse of energy, and the valley-like bottom is the pause, known as the trough. In other words, the frequencies are determined by how close together or far apart (or how frequently, if you will) these waves occur. The range of wave-like radiant light energy frequencies is referred to as the electromagnetic spectrum of which our special senses can only perceive a small percentage. Some frequency waves are beyond the range that our special senses are able to detect. That is, the wavelengths are either too long, such as radio waves, or too short, like ultraviolet rays (think of a sunburn – you can see its effect but not the invisible energy that creates the event due to its high-frequency wavelengths – waves that are consequently very close together and considered short wavelengths). I know this may sound confusing.

Understand that the frequency of a wave is inversely proportional to its wavelength. That means that waves with a high frequency have a short wavelength, while waves with a low frequency have a longer wavelength. Beliefs also fall into this category. That's right! Beliefs as well as the feelings, thoughts, and the emotions generated by them have energy and are composed of matter.

The closer together the vibrational frequencies, the higher the vibration and the higher the energy. Understand, the only reason you cannot see magnetic energy is that the wavelengths are too close together (short wavelengths). By the way, your thought wavelengths are even shorter. Listen, the only reason you can see different colors is due to their wavelengths. You can see the color red because its wavelengths are neither too short nor too long (for example, infra-red cannot be seen because it has a longer wavelength than the color red). Again, thoughts are energy, which can cause vibrational influences. Now, consider the fact that scientists have discovered that energy can travel at the speed of light (186,000 miles per second).

Therefore, thoughts being energy can also travel at that speed, which can be a good rationale for the concept of Remote Healing, which I will discuss shortly. Hopefully, this explanation was not too esoteric and afforded you a better insight and appreciation concerning my soon-to-be-discussed concept on intentional love and healing in the following chapter.

There have been clinicians over the years who have developed methods that delve into the relationship between the workings of the conscious mind and vibrational frequencies with gratifying clinical results through the use of a technique known as applied kinesiology. One that comes to mind is Dr. John Diamond, a psychiatrist who used applied kinesiology to diagnose and treat his patients.

First, let's briefly explore the history and development of this dynamic diagnostic tool.

Without going into too much detail, in the early 1970s, a chiropractor named George Goodheart discovered a unique muscle testing technique. He found that specific muscles in the body were connected to specific organs. For example, the teres muscle, located adjacent to the posterior aspect of the shoulder, relates to the function of the thyroid gland. He then determined that testing the strength of a particular muscle, in this case, the teres muscle, could reveal whether that connecting organ was in a state of health or one of pathology. In other words, if the thyroid, as mentioned earlier gland were in a pathological state, the muscle would test as being weak. Conversely, he then further determined that a healthy thyroid would manifest by a strong teres muscle when tested. It also should be noted that Dr. Goodheart found that the muscles went weak immediately when exposed to any substance the body sensed to be detrimental to its homeostasis (balanced state of health).

Individual muscles were also found to be associated with specific acupuncture meridians. Suppose you would like to have a better understanding of this wonderful technique. In that case, you can buy a book by Dr. David S. Walther, *Applied Kinesiology Synopsis* (I had the good fortune to meet the inimitable Dr. Goodheart in the early 1970's at one of his teaching seminars, where he used me as a test subject for demonstration purposes, treating me successfully for a chronic misaligned carpal bone in my wrist).

Although this amazing technique, from a diagnostic standpoint, has been proven to be very accurate by laboratory blood test and acupuncture and has been accepted among professionals from many different disciplines, to date, it has never been completely accepted by mainstream medicine, which is why I feel it necessary to elaborate on the efficacy of this wonderful diagnostic tool.

Hopefully, now you will come to realize this is not some "hocus pocus" technique, but in fact, an extremely reliable and well-researched diagnostic tool that was used as means to prove the efficacy of thought vibrations as they relate to one's state of mind. It is gratifying to note that today applied kinesiology is being used extensively by holistic-oriented physicians.

We said earlier that everything in the universe vibrates, including our thoughts. Therefore, to complete this discussion on thought and vibration, I will try to put this concept into its proper context regarding health and wellness. In his book, *Thought Vibrations*, William Atkinson discusses the impact of thought vibrations on one's life. He states how we know that the universe is governed by law, that "it has many manifestations, but only the one law. We are familiar with some of these manifestations but unaware of others, although we are becoming more aware of these manifestations every day. The veil is being gradually lifted. For example, it is very common to hear people refer to the Law of Gravity but, for the most part, ignore the manifestation of the Law of Attraction in the thought world.

We recognize the powers of the law that heavenly bodies affect the earth (i.e., the Moon affects ocean tides), and the manifestation that holds the revolving planets in their respective orbits, but we close our eyes to the mighty Law that draws to us the things that we desire or fear that can either make or mar our lives. When we come to realize that our thoughts are a force, yes, a manifestation of energy, having a magnetic power of attraction, we will begin to understand the whys and wherefores of many things that up until now have escaped our understanding. No study will so well repay a student for his time and trouble as this study of the workings of this mighty law of the world of thought known as the Law of Attraction.

When we think, we send out our vibrations of a fine ethereal substance which are as real as the vibrations manifesting light, heat, magnetism, and electricity. That these vibrations are not evident to your special senses is not proof that they do not exist. A powerful magnet will send out vibrations and exert a force sufficient enough to attract a piece of steel weighing possibly one hundred pounds to itself, but we can neither see, taste, hear, smell, nor feel the mighty force."

Similarly, thought vibrations cannot be perceived by our senses (however, there are on record those who are peculiarly sensitive to psychic impressions which have perceived powerful thought waves), yet many of us can testify that there are times when we are thinking of something, and someone nearby verbalizes exactly what we were thinking. How do you think that happens? Well, someone is picking up the thought vibrations you are transmitting, with one of you even innocently commenting, “We must be on the same wavelength.” So true.

Why is it that some people give you “bad vibes?” I submit to you that you are picking up their low vibratory "attractor field" due to their undesirable state of consciousness (if inclined, the reader can refer to Dr. Hawkins’ book, *Power Vs. Force,* in which there is a chart he developed, “The Map of Consciousness,” for additional insight and understanding of this phenomenon).

In this work by Dr. Hawkins, he mentions a 20-year worldwide research study he conducted with colleagues that calibrated different states of consciousness and their corresponding vibrational levels. The modality used for testing subjects was the previously explained muscle testing (Applied Kinesiology). This research showed that the higher one's state of consciousness, the higher and stronger their level of vibration. For example, a person who manifests a love state of consciousness will vibrate much higher than someone in a constant apathy state. Again, if interested, you can go to veritaspub.com and order "The Map of Consciousness," which describes all the different states of consciousness and their corresponding vibratory levels plus additional corresponding traits of the different levels of consciousness.

Light and heat are manifested by vibration levels of a far lower intensity than those of thought, which enable them to be observed by our senses. The annals of science cast an interesting light upon this. In his work, Professor M.M. Williams, "Short Chapters in Science," says, “There is no gradation between the most rapid undulations or trembling that produce our sensation of sound and the slowest of those which give rise to our sensations of gentle warmth. There is a huge gap between them. Wide enough to include another world of motion, all lying between our world of sound and our world of heat and light, and there is no good reason whatever for supposing that matter is incapable of such intermediate activity or that such activity may not give rise to intermediate sensations, provided there are organs taking up and sensifying their movements."

An interesting concept when considering the notion of thought vibrations, is it not? Williams continues, "We often heard the well-known mental science statement, *thoughts are things*, and we say these words without consciously realizing just what is the meaning of the statement. If we truly comprehend the truth of this statement and the natural consequences of the truth in back of it, we should understand many things which have appeared dark to us and would be able to use this wonderful power (thought force), just as we use any other manifestation of energy. Listen, when we think, we set into motion vibrations of a very high degree and just as real as the vibrations of light, heat, sound, and electricity. When we understand the laws governing the production and transmissions of these vibrations, we will be able to use them in our daily lives, just as we do the better-known forms of energy."

These authorities are cited to give you food for thought and demonstrate that thought vibrations exist – that this fact has been fully established to the satisfaction of numerous investigators of this subject. A little reflection will make you aware that it coincides with your own experiences.

Perhaps, before leaving this topic on vibrations, which may be a new concept to many readers, further discussion on how different vibrations can positively impact your body is indicated. So, let me elaborate.

Vibrations from Sound and Their Effects on Healing

The practice of using Sound vibrations for healing is not a revolutionary concept. Actually, it has been in existence for thousands of years. It has ancient roots in many cultures from all over the globe. A classic example would be the Aboriginal tribes in Australia, who are known to use the Didgeridoo as a sound healing instrument via its vibrations for over tens of thousands of years. Likewise, the Tibetan monks in the Himalayas use the vibrations from singing bowls to attain a higher state of consciousness during their spiritual ceremonies. A more modern well-known application for the use of sound for healing is the use of ultrasound to break up masses such as stones via pulsed frequencies, which produce a particular vibration to break down the mass. It is also used in some hospitals now, in the form of music, before surgery for relaxation and afterward to enhance recovery.

I had the good fortune to study in Switzerland and Spain, and Malibu, California, under the guidance of a brilliant researcher, Fabien Maman, in the field of sound and its relationship to healing for two years. He is listed in Webster's New Encyclopedia 1993 as "The Father of Sound Therapy."

Although many different applications of sound therapy were presented by this brilliant man, being an acupuncturist, I was very interested in a particular therapy being taught. Eventually, I became certified in his therapeutic system based on the concepts of Traditional Chinese Medicine. That is the use of special tuning forks with their particular vibrational frequencies on specific acupuncture points. This approach breaks up energy blockages in the acupuncture pathways to rebalance the body's energy for healing many different afflictions. Treating patients with this new system was a very gratifying experience (not to mention patients appreciating the application of tuning forks rather than the traditional acupuncture needles).

Vibrations from Refractive Light (Colors) and Their Relationship to Healing

I had mentioned earlier that Traditional Chinese Medicine teaches us that different emotions resonate with different organs of the body via our vibrational frequencies (i.e., anger dominates the Liver). Understand, the body-mind connection, including your emotions and spirit that we have been discussing, is intertwined like a web with all other aspects of Traditional Chinese Medicine, including bodily organs. Human beings are considered a microcosm of the universe in the energetic Chinese system of healing and, consequently, in a relationship with Nature.

Therefore, since you are a reflection of Nature which is composed of colors, being that reflection, so too are you composed of colors. Just like your emotions can relate to specific organs, the same can be said for certain colors. For example, White (which is a combination of red, green, and blue) has a wavelength producing a frequency that resonates with the Lung's vibrational frequency; Blue/Black resonates with the Kidneys; Green resonates with the Liver, Yellow (a combination of green and red) resonates with the Spleen; and Red resonates with the Heart.

Each time you choose clothing to wear, or decorate a certain room in your home, enjoy any form of visual art, or even select a certain food to eat, you are interacting and resonating with different wavelengths of light (colors). Research has shown that different selections of color decorations and lighting make a huge difference in the behavior of psychiatric hospital patients. This concept of the effects of color on the body may seem foreign to most; however, when you understand the interplay of different emotions and colors due to their resonance with different vibrations from their respective wavelengths, you can begin to have a better understanding and appreciation for color therapy.

Again, this discussion is intended, without getting too esoteric, to be a general, brief overview of the concept of color therapy. If the reader is fascinated with this modality and desires to learn more, there are many good books on this subject.

Hopefully, this brief introduction to the use of color as another healing modality will open your mind to appreciate the application of this modality as another alternative means of healing.

Creative Visualization

Gandhi once said, "You must be the change you wish to see in the world." Very profound, but how can we attain such a goal? Well, the best tool I know of to accomplish such an altruistic goal is to act as if you have already made such an admirable change in yourself. You see, my friend, someone once said, "To become, act as if."

In other words, since we now know that action follows thought, acting as if you already possess a particular attribute, or have achieved any other goal for that matter, instills confidence which leads to improved self-esteem, which in turn leads to more confidence creating this positive attitude which becomes part of your belief system.

Creative Visualization is, creating a mental picture that can be employed to facilitate making a goal a reality. This technique uses the power of your imagination to create what you want in your life.

Not only must you see yourself in your mind's eye to be acting in a desired way, but also by incorporating all of your special senses when trying to visualize your life's dreams. For example, if your goal is to be more of a picture of health, make a mental picture of yourself performing your daily activities of living, employing a healthy lifestyle through the use of your imagination.

Notice what color apron you are wearing while creating a nutritious meal in your kitchen, try to feel the heat emanating from your stove, hear the birds singing outside your window, smell the delicious aroma of the meal being prepared, and feel how happy you are after creating such a delicious dinner. The more vivid and clear the mental picture you create, the more it becomes ingrained as part of your belief system. There are records of individuals diagnosed with advanced debilitating diseases who, unbelievably, have been totally healed solely through the use of creative visualization. "Spontaneous remission" is the term used by western medicine when such a phenomenon occurs.

Listen, this concept is not new. The Soviets used this technique in the 1970s to compete in sports. Also, studies show brain patterns being activated, similar to athletes physically practicing a particular feat using this technique. In fact, many well-known athletes use creative visualization before engaging in their particular sport. I highly recommend practicing this technique. If you want to be all that you can be, you can, especially where your health is concerned.

In conclusion, I hope that in sharing the writings of some brilliant pioneers in the scientific field of Quantum Physics, and this additional information on vibrations and their relationship with sound and color, I have shed enough light on this phenomenon of thought and vibration that you will have a better understanding, and, yes, even a belief in the ability of your thoughts to have a definite impact on your behavior, and, consequently, your health.

The following chapter will discuss my concept of how the body can heal with "Intentional Love."

Chapter Eight

Intentional Love and Healing

I mentioned earlier that no doctor anywhere has ever healed anything. The plaque in my wellness center's waiting room said, "God Does the Healing; the Doctor Collects the Fee." However, it wasn't until I read a book, *Light on the Path,* by the Yogi Baba Muktananda, that added a dimension to my treatment of patients. In my search for self-development, I attended a weekend retreat at one of his centers in South Fallsburg, New York, in the mid-'80s.

The retreat, led by two of his disciples, focused on meditation and chanting, which I found very peaceful. During one of the intermissions, I went to the bookstore and bought this book, *Light on the Path*, which really resonated with me and made my retreat worthwhile. In one chapter, he discussed how to be a better instrument of healing, explaining that professionals in the healing arts are only facilitators for healing, which I strongly believed. But what really struck me was the emphasis he put on the veneration of the person being treated. He suggested before treating a patient to think of someone you held in high esteem (for me, it is Jesus Christ), and imagine you were treating that person—a phenomenon I refer to as intentional love.

When I began practicing this concept through the process of visualization with patients, I believe I became more of a vessel to be used by a higher power to facilitate at least a partial or sometimes even complete permanent remission of someone's condition (I also observed that when I was too busy and feeling overwhelmed, or my ego would get in the way, which happened more than I would like to admit, I would fail to be present as I should, and my results were not as successful). I truly believe someone can be prayed over, or even just prayed for, and have healing due to this intentional love for the person.

In addition, my studies in acupuncture school taught me that all sickness and disease could be related to an imbalance of energy in the body. Too much energy in one area, like a traffic jam, can lead to pain initially (this phenomenon in Chinese medicine is referred to as "chi stagnation") and, if not corrected, leads to more serious maladies. Conversely, a deficiency of energy, which, more often than not, is a more chronic condition, usually due to a long-standing excess of stagnant energy, can yield weakness and fatigue initially and eventually lead to a more severe condition if not corrected (known as "chi deficiency"). Once the energy in the body is balanced, either through an acupuncture treatment or herbs that may have either a cooling or warming effect, depending on the diagnosis, or any other energetic modality for that matter, the patient usually has a marked, speedy recovery.

In addition, I explained earlier that everything in the universe has a particular vibration, including our thoughts and feelings. Research has proven that the higher one's state of consciousness (one's thoughts), the higher and more forceful their vibration potential. I believe that well-intentioned healers resonate at a higher state of consciousness (consequently being imbued with this stronger vibrational force), which enables them to be conduits of healing through the grace of God due to their sincere, pure intentions.

In other words, when intentional love is applied, it optimizes the potential for the facilitator. Usually, it is a professional in the healing arts. He can use his God-given talent to become a conduit or a vessel that can assimilate and transmit a high, powerful vibration of the love of God to a compromised individual via the phenomenon of resonance. Resonance occurs when two forces meet with matching frequency of vibration—in this case, the vibrations between the love of God and the conscious state of the intentional love of the facilitator. Research tells us that a higher vibrational frequency will yield an increase in its force and speed.

That, I believe in my heart, is a manifestation of the grace of God. I also theorize that this higher frequency, when transmitted through the well-intentioned facilitator, can potentially unblock and eventually balance the energy in the body of the compromised individual for the potential healing, through the grace of God, to take place.

I hypothesize that through the phenomenon of intentional loving prayers, the laying-on of hands is not necessarily a prerequisite for potential healing to take place. It is a fact that many people have even been healed through the gift of God's grace without any physical intervention, which has been referred to as a miracle or spontaneous healing.

In Matthew 18:20, he quotes Jesus saying, “for where two or three are gathered together in my name, there am I in the midst of them.” Regardless of its interpretation by theologians, this quote has a special meaning to my heart. You see, as previously mentioned, I think prayers are a form of intentional love. When performed in a group of two or more to pray for healing, I believe He is present “in the midst of them” and can intercede to make one's healing a reality, which I believe is commonly referred to as “a spontaneous remission.”

A perfect example of such a phenomenon took place concerning one of my daughters. Many years ago, she had a positive pap smear (cancer cells were found in her cervix) and was scheduled for a biopsy of the region. She went to a Catholic Healing Mass where the priest said there was someone at the Mass who was being healed of cancer of the cervix. My daughter's friend, who was also attending this healing Mass, encouraged my daughter to claim the healing, which my daughter then accepted, though she did not expect to heal. During the initial consultation, the doctor was emphatic and insisted that a biopsy was necessary since her Pap smear report indicated the presence of cancer cells in her cervical tissue. However, upon a thorough examination, he was surprised and, in fact, quite amazed at his observation, stating, “This is the healthiest and pinkest cervix I have ever seen, and I cannot bring myself to biopsy it.” At that moment, my daughter suddenly recalled the healing Mass from a few weeks prior and thought, "Oh, Wow! I must have been healed." In fact, she *was* healed, having normal test results ever since, for over 25 years. Thanks be to God!

I believe having intentional love via prayer for a loved one can also elicit healing from a long distance. How is that possible, you might ask? Well, without getting too technical, in Quantum Physics, there is a phenomenon known as "entanglement," which Albert Einstein explained as "Objects that can become linked and instantaneously influence one another regardless of the distance between them." (Einstein referred to this elusive phenomenon, which baffled him until the day he died, as "spooky action at a distance," since it seemed incompatible with elements of his Special Theory of Relativity). I surmise that this phenomenon of "entanglement" is made possible because energy, substantiated by research through Quantum Physics, underlies all matter and can never be separated, even though the particles of matter might be. (Interestingly enough, I just happened to notice an article—published as I wrote these words, on July 13, 2019—by the journal, *Science Advances*, entitled, "Imaging Bell-Type Non-Local Behavior," which discusses how, for the first time, scientists at the University of Glasgow, Scotland, captured images with a special camera, of entangled photons, which are particles representing a quantum of light, making visible the "spookiness" referred to by Einstein concerning entanglement. Now that is what I call serendipitous!)

We are all connected through this ubiquitous energy that underpins all matter (which includes the human species). Therefore, I believe it is through this medium of "entangled energy," if you will, in which all matter is interconnected. Therefore there is the potential for healing vibrations of intentional love (i.e., prayer) to be transmitted instantaneously to someone, regardless of the distance of separation, since we are, like I said, all connected through energy (by the way, scientists claim that entanglement can transfer information (i.e., thought vibrations) at a rate at least the speed of light, which travels at the speed of 186,000 mi. per second. Some experts believe even faster, which, to my knowledge, has not been proven at the time of this writing, which could explain how sometimes a healing can take place quite rapidly, regardless of the distance from where this intentional love originates from.

Unfortunately, having the most loving intentions for a loved one sometimes fails to have the desired results due to the limitations of matter. According to Dr. Bernie Siegel in his book *Love, Medicines, and Miracles*, he states that he feels the ability to heal is to give unconditional love and be open to accepting it. I agree with him. For example, a person might have low self-worth, and they don't feel worthy of any prayers or good intentions. This is all left up to conjecture.

I realize this concept will be foreign to the thinking of most presently. However, I ask the reader to consider the fact that, in the time of Christ, phenomena that have come to fruition today were probably just as foreign (i.e., holding a device that could communicate with someone halfway around the world, or even landing on the Moon, for that matter). In my way of thinking, this concept of entanglement is a rationale I can accept to attempt to explain, via the grace of God, this phenomenon of healing. Hopefully, this interpretation on my part concerning healing will provide some food for thought to the open-minded.

This concept of healing, especially from a distance, is not as foreign an idea as the reader might think. There are many healers today who practice healing from a distance and refer to it as Remote Healing. In this chapter, I simply attempt to explain my humble opinion of the mechanism by which, through the Grace of God, such a phenomenon can take place. Dr. Deepak Chopra, in his book, *Quantum Healing*, discusses a study regarding the topic of healing from a distance:

> "Especially intriguing is a pioneering study of native Hawaiian healers led by the late Dr. Jeanne Achterberg, a physiologist of the mind-body connection who was fascinated by the anecdotes that native healers often did

their work from a distance. Here is how the Achterberg study worked, as described in *Super Brain*, which I wrote with Rudolph F. Tanzi.

> In 2005, after a two-year search, she and her colleagues gathered 11 Hawaiian healers. Each had pursued their native healing tradition for an average of 23 years. The healers were asked to select a person with whom they had successfully worked in the past and with whom they felt an empathetic connection. This person would be the recipient of healing in a controlled setting. The healers described their methods in a variety of ways – as prayer, sending energy, good intentions, or simply thinking or wishing the highest good for their subjects. Achterberg simply called these efforts distant intentionality (DI).
>
> Each subject was isolated from the healer while undergoing an MRI of their brain activity. The healers were asked to send DI at two-minute intervals randomly: the individuals could not have anticipated when the DI was being sent. Yet their brains did. Significant differences were found between the experimental (send) periods and control (no send) periods in 10 out of 11 cases. For the send periods, specific areas within the subjects' brains "lit up" on the MRI scan, indicating increased metabolic activity. This did not occur during the no send period."

Let me try to open your mind a little more. In his book, *The Spontaneous Healing of Belief*, the brilliant Gregg Braden designed an excellent flow chart when discussing the relationship between our beliefs and the changes they create in the physical world. If I can paraphrase his flow chart, it goes something like this:

"All the atoms of matter are formed by electrical and magnetic energy = if the energy changes, then the atoms change = the heart produces the strongest electrical, and magnetic energy of the body = Heart-based feelings/beliefs create electrical and magnetic energy in the form of waves that extend into the world beyond our bodies = as we change our beliefs, we change the energy that forms the atoms of our world."

Listen, from an energy perspective you can now appreciate the saying, "If you change the way you look at things, the things you look at change."

Also, when a doctor looks at an EKG, he is looking at what?

WAVES!

And, yes, your heart puts out 60 times more energy than your brain when an EKG is compared to the brain measurement of an EEG. Gregg goes on to explain, "Clearly, science doesn't have all of the answers regarding precisely how our beliefs affect reality. If it did, we'd obviously be living in a very different world. However, what science does tell us for certain is that our hearts are quite literally at the core of the electrical and magnetic fields that communicate with the organs within us. Studies also show that our heart fields are not limited to the inside of our bodies. In fact, they have been measured to extend distances as great as eight feet beyond our bodies."

Gregg goes on to point out that when asked why only eight feet, the researchers said that number resulted from a limitation in their equipment to measure such a field. They then admitted, in all probability, that it extends for distances of miles beyond the original place where the heart resides.

Okay, let's try to connect some dots here. It has been established that thoughts, just like beliefs, are waves of energy, and therefore, just like our beliefs, they can extend far beyond the borders of our bodies. Therefore, is it that much of a stretch to believe that, through the phenomenon of unconditional intentional thoughts of love, healing energy, through the grace of God, can be transmitted in the form of energy waves (just as radio waves are transmitted to other receivers at another radio station), to rearrange the atoms of matter in a sick person for healing to take place?

In my heart, I believe this could be a rationale to explain spontaneous remissions and, yes, even miracles through God's grace.

Part Two: Suggestions for a Healthier Lifestyle

At this time, I would like to share with you some suggestions on how to have a more balanced lifestyle. Understanding and realizing we are a complex species requires addressing this spiritual, emotional/mental, biochemical, and physical plane. In other words, we need to take a holistic approach to this worthwhile challenge. To ignore this concept will surely result in our falling short of the goal of making our journey through life a much healthier and indeed a much happier one. Therefore, let us attempt to address this challenge with suggestions for each level separately.

Chapter Nine

Spiritual Plane

Someone once asked the great spiritual leader of India, Mahatma Gandhi, "What is the secret to happiness?" Without much deliberation, Gandhi told the disciple, "If you truly want to be happy, you should serve others." Very simple yet profound advice. So, help others in any way you can. Pick an organization or a cause you really believe in and volunteer. Doing good for others comes back many times over. It goes without saying it should be acted out of love without expecting some reciprocity or reward. I believe performing these acts of love will only serve to raise one's state of consciousness, resulting in a higher state of vibration, which, as previously mentioned, was quantified by the work of Dr. Hawkins. I believe the higher our state of consciousness, and consequently our vibratory force, the happier and healthier we become as we are mindful and aware to try to make ourselves one with our fellow man. This can be accomplished by being the first to love through the action of gladly serving the other in that present moment.

Realize that the present moment is where life dwells and, consequently, the only time when you are in control. Listen, it has been said, "Yesterday is history, tomorrow is a mystery, today is a gift, which is why we call it the present." I promise you, if you try being more aware and mindful with a present-time consciousness, it will create more quality, and, yes, meaning in your life, which I believe we are all striving for.

By the way, we can become more mindful through meditation, which has many well-known health benefits. In fact, in his book, *Quantum Healing*, Dr. Deepak Chopra mentions that it is now known that there are even more holistic benefits achieved through the practice of meditation. To quote Dr. Chopra, here are the benefits:

"Promotes overall balance or homeostasis.

Moves easily through the system, without destruction or blockages.

Generates new neural pathways.

Promotes the production of new brain cells.

Improves gene expression.

Allows every cell to function normally, without anomalies or aberrant behavior.

Supports the immune system, increasing resistance to disease.

Counteracts the effects over time of entropy (the using up of energy) and aging.

Increases a sense of wellbeing: the person feels healthy, vibrant, and alive."

Now that you know all these additional benefits from meditation elucidated by Dr. Chopra, hopefully, it will motivate you to experience this wonderful phenomenon yourself. There are many classes available for student participation. Contacting a local Yoga center would be a good starting point.

Also, we have been told by the sages to have an *attitude of gratitude*. When you awake in the morning, before you get out of bed, thank God for your life and for giving you "one more day." Focus on being thankful for all that is good in your life, rather than any challenges you may have. Remember, things can always be worse, and you were never promised a rose garden, so lose any feelings of entitlement or victimhood you may be harboring. There is an old American Indian saying that puts this concept concerning Gratitude into its proper perspective. "When you arise in the morning, give thanks to the morning light, give thanks for life and strength, give thanks for your food, give thanks for the joy of living, and if, perchance, you see no reason to give thanks, rest assured the fault is yours."

Here is another story that I feel also brings home this point:

The Man and His Cross

A man who felt his burdens and problems in life was too much of a cross to carry that he carried the weight of the world on his shoulders.

One night, after saying his evening prayers, he fell asleep and had a dream that changed his whole perspective on life. You see, in the dream, he went up to heaven and talked to God.

During his conversation with God, he mentioned that his Cross was too much to bear, and he asked if there was something that God could do for him to "lighten his load." Well, in the dream, God assured him his wish would be granted and told the man to go through a doorway that suddenly appeared before him. Then he was told to put his Cross down and pick out a new one that he felt would be much easier for him to bear.

When he entered the room, he noticed that this was no ordinary room. It contained miles and miles of different-sized crosses. Well, you can imagine, the man spent hours going through all the different crosses until he found a tiny little cross that he believed was the answer to all his problems. So, he exchanged the crosses, thanked God for being so understanding, and returned home a very happy man.

Now, in the dream, a few years went by, and, wouldn't you know it, his new cross was getting to be too much to bear. Well, you guessed it! He went back to see God once more, explaining that the cross that he exchanged his first cross for was now too much of a burden, and he asked once again if he could exchange this cross for a smaller one. God agreed and allowed him to again enter the room with all the different-sized crosses, so he could hopefully find an even smaller cross to exchange. This time around, he spent days to find a smaller cross, being persistent in his quest to find the perfect cross he believed would be the answer to his prayers. Finally, he found this cross that was so small he almost did not notice it, so he immediately exchanged the crosses. Feeling grateful, he once again went to see God to thank Him for being so kind. However, when he approached God with the cross he picked out, God asked him if he was sure that this was the cross he wanted. The man assured God that this was the perfect cross for him and asked why God questioned his choice. God then exclaimed, "My son, this is the Cross you brought here originally when you first came to see Me, explaining it was too much to bear." He immediately woke up and realized he should be thankful for what he has and how fortunate he was compared to others.

Hopefully, this was a lesson learned. Also, try not to take your life for granted. Someone once said people make plans, and God laughs as if it is a given that you will still be around in the next moment, let alone in the near future. So, ask yourself, *Are you living in the present?* Quite often, we worry about things we did in the past or fret about things that might happen in the future, all the while missing out on life's greatest gift—the present! It is so important to be in the present moment completely. After all, none of us can know if we will be here tomorrow, but often we are worried about what might happen down the road. Go for it and try to be present in every moment, so you get the most out of life (much easier said than done but also worth it). Please don't miss the joy of life by wasting energy thinking about the past or worrying about the future.
The following story emphasizes that point.

The Man and the Mirror Planet

There once was another man who had a dream. In this dream, he traveled by molecular transport to another planet. Remarkably, this planet was a mirror image of the planet Earth. There were automobiles and shopping centers identical to those on Earth. Social media was also quite popular, as well as television. The list of identicals he observed continued until one night he was watching television as he would so often do on planet Earth, seeing all his favorite sitcoms. Then the news came on at 11 p.m., just like on Earth. At the end of the news report, just like what would normally take place on Earth, the weatherman gave the weather report. However, at the end of the weather report, before breaking for a commercial like on Earth, the weatherman said something very odd. He mentioned to stay tuned for the local Anxiety report. Well, as you can imagine, this statement by the television announcer got the earthling's attention. Quite understandably, the next morning, after listening to this abstract type report, he made an appointment with the woman at the television station who gave this very interesting and insightful report. At their meeting, they spent the time comparing different concepts and how they were addressed on their respective planet. Eventually, they discussed the feeling of worry. The earthling asked the woman how they addressed the phenomenon of worry on her planet. "Oh, that's simple," said the woman. “We just put on our anti- worry vest.” The earthling looked confused, so she elaborated. She said if you were worried about something you might have forgotten to do or would like to change some action you felt uncomfortable about, or conversely worried about something that might happen in the future. You would just put on this anti-worry vest which would take you to the moment in time you were concerned about and take care of the perceived problem. She then explained that once the concern was addressed, whether in the past or the future. The anti-worry vest would then be removed to bring the person back to the present moment, allowing the person to resume their carefree life. Needless to say, the earthling was flabbergasted. The reporter then proceeded to ask him how they dealt with worry on Earth. The man was hesitant initially, then proclaimed that there was no such means on the planet Earth to be able to do anything about worry. The woman looking puzzled with his response, then asked, "You mean you really can't do anything about worry on your planet?”

“That is correct,” he responded. She then retorted, "Then why, my friend, do you worry?"

Enough said.

It is also recommended to start your day with a few minutes of meditation or prayer, asking your higher power for guidance in keeping you more mindful and intent on being the first to love whomever you encounter that day. I believe that striving for this higher state of consciousness will result in what the Bible refers to as being paid back a "hundred-fold," experiencing a much happier and, consequently, healthier life. Also, practice being detached from whatever life events are presented to you, whether good or bad, realizing they are temporary, having an attitude of "This, too, shall pass." Try to avoid practicing what Dale Carnegie called the three "Cs" in his book, *How to Win Friends and Influence People:* Criticizing, Condemning, and Complaining. It is a total waste of energy and has a negative impact on others. Finally, do not judge others. We all have shortcomings. Usually, the fault you see in others is a reflection of your misgivings. There is a story in the Bible where a violent crowd was about to stone a woman of ill repute, and Jesus intervened, exclaiming, "Let he who is without sin cast the first stone," causing the crowd to drop the stones and walk away with their heads down. It is said that when you point the finger at someone, you have three more fingers pointing back at you. So, keep a smile on your face and be the first to love. It takes fewer muscles to smile than it does to grimace. As St. Teresa of Calcutta said, "...a smile is the beginning of love."

Hopefully, some of these concepts will become part of your daily life if they have not already, and they will help guide you on your Spiritual Path.

Chapter Ten

Words of Wisdom

To encourage the serious reader on the path of this exciting journey towards a spiritual enlightenment, I have taken the liberty of including some "words of wisdom" in the form of quotes and sayings from Masters and Sages of Spirituality to aid in inspiring you to be your best self through these deep reflective words. There are 52 of these beautiful quotes. I recommend taking one per week, reading them while really focusing on their meaning. Try digesting them first thing in the morning and once at night to become imbued and hopefully inspired by their concepts. There are no iron-clad rules here; please just follow your heart. You may find certain sayings that resonate with you more than others, so feel free to choose your favorite ones and focus on them as you prefer. It is no coincidence that about half these sayings are taken from Taoist Master Lao Tzu. He lived in approximately 500 BC, and he is considered one of the wisest men ever to have walked the Earth.

Interestingly enough, the great teacher, Confucius, known for creating ethical standards for family and public interactions and education, also lived during this same period. As legend would have it, there was a constant arguing among Lao Tzu's and Confucius' disciples about who was the wisest in the land. The legend continues, saying these two great teachers were finally brought together to discuss different concepts about life. They went up into the mountains for isolation and deliberation and were not heard from for several months. When they finally descended the mountain and met with their disciples, Confucius supposedly said, "I went to the mountain top and have met the dragon." (In Chinese folklore, the dragon is a symbol of great power).

Here, then, are these reflective words of wisdom. Try reading them, paying attention, and assimilating these profound words into your life. Enjoy!

Many of these sayings and quotes are taken from *The Zen Book of*

Life by Mark Zocchi, and *Heart of a Buddha* from Amitabha Publications.

1. "Out of clutter, find simplicity.
From discord, find harmony.
In the middle of difficulty
Lies opportunity."
~ Albert Einstein

2. "Do not dwell in the past.
Do not dream of the future.
Concentrate the mind
On the present moment."
~ The Buddha

3. "The more you have,
The more it has you"
~ Lao Tzu

4. "If you really know how to live,
What better way to start the day
Than with a smile?
Smiling helps you approach the day
With gentleness and understanding.
Smile with your whole Being."
~ Thich Nhat Hanh

5. "When you arise in the morning
Give thanks for life and strength
Give thanks for your food
Give thanks for the joy of living,
And if, perchance, you see no reason to give thanks,
Rest assured the fault is yours"
~ American Indian Saying

6. "When you can be calm
in the midst of activity

This is the true state of nature.
When you can be happy
In the midst of hardship,
Then you see the true potential of the mind"
~ Hauchu Daoren

7. "Know things like this:
A mirage, a cloud castle…
Nothing appears as it is."
~ The Buddha

8. "If you laugh at misfortune,
You will not be overcome by it"
~ Valluvar

9. "Do not pursue the past
Do not lose yourself in the future
The past is no longer
The future is yet to come
Look very deeply at life as it is,
Here and Now.
The practitioner dwells in stability and freedom."
~ Bhaddekaratta Sutta

10. "To abandon what is harmful,
To adopt what is wholesome,
To purify the heart and mind,
This is the teaching of the Buddha."
~ The Buddha

11. "I have three things to teach:
Simplicity, patience, and compassion.
These three are your great treasures.
Simple action and in thought,
You return to the source of being.
Patience with both friends and enemies
You accord with the way things are.

Compassion toward yourself,
You reconcile all beings in the world."
~ Lao Tzu
Tao Te Ching

12. "Breathing in, I calm body and mind. Breathing out, I smile.
Dwelling in the present moment I know this is the only moment."
~ Thich Nhat Hahn

13. "Within your own house swells the treasure of joy,
So why do you go begging door-to-door?"
~ Sufi Saying

14. "In the pursuit of knowledge,
Every day something is gained.
In the pursuit of freedom,
Every day something is let go"
~ Tao Te Ching

15. "We cannot always fix every event distress,
But can always be present, awake,
And receive each moment with
Compassion and simplicity."
~ Christina Feldman

16. "Mindfulness is a shortcut to happiness."
~ Buddhist Monk

17. "Hear what is said,
Retain what is important,
Speak what is worthy,
Attach to nothing."
~ The Buddha

18. "We are what we think.

All that we are arises with our thoughts.
With our thoughts we make the world.
Speak or act with an impure mind,
And trouble will find you
As the wheel follows the Ox that draws the cart.
We are what we think.
All that we are arises in our thoughts.
With our thoughts we make the world.
Speak or act with a pure mind,
And happiness will follow you
As your shadow, unshakeable."
~ The Dhammapadda

19. "If you are patient in one moment of anger,
You will escape a hundred days of sorrow."
~ Chinese Proverb

20. "Speaking pleasant words
without practicing them
is like a fine flower
without fragrance."
~ The Buddha

21. "By letting it go, it all gets done.
The world is won by those who let it go.
But, when you try and try,
The world is beyond the winning."
~ Lao Tzu

22. "The best person is like water.
Water is good; it benefits all things
And does not compete with them.
It dwells in lonely places that all disdain."
~ Tao Te Ching

23. "The softest things in the world
Overcome the hardest things in the world."

~ Lao Tzu

24. "The best soldier does not attack.
The superior fighter succeeds without violence.
The greatest conqueror wins without struggle.
The most successful manager leads
Without dictating."
~ Tao Te Ching

25. "He who grasps, loses."
~ Lao Tzu

26. "Life is a series of natural
And spontaneous changes.
Don't resist them—that only creates sorrow.
Let reality be reality.
Let things flow naturally forward
In whatever way they will."
~ Tao Te Ching

27. "What the caterpillar calls the end,
The rest of the world calls the butterfly."
~ Lao Tzu

28. "A tree that is unbending is easily broken."
~ Lao Tzu

29. "When I let go of who I am,
I become who I might be."
~ Lao Tzu

30. "To become, act as if."
~ W. Clement Stone

31. "Manifest plainness, embrace
Simplicity, reduce selfishness,
Have few desires."
~ Lao Tzu

32. “Silence is the source of great strength.”
~ Lao Tzu

33. “Whenever you hear that someone
Else has been successful, rejoice.
Always practice rejoicing for others—
Whether your friend or enemy.
If you cannot practice rejoicing,
No matter how long you live,
You will not be happy.”
~Lama Zopa Rinpoche

34. “Adversity brings with it
Seeds of equal or better benefits.”
~ W. Clement Stone

35. “To the mind that is still,
The whole universe surrenders.”
~ Lao Tzu

36. “We can find ourselves leaning into the
Future that has not arrived,
Or leaning back into the past that
Has long gone.
This is the very moment that we
Can calmly stand in the moment,
Letting go of our resistance on the
Breath and softening our warm hearts.”
~ MZ

37. “Every time you smile at someone,
It is an action of love, a gift to that
person, a beautiful thing.”
~ St. Teresa of Calcutta

38. “The journey of a thousand miles
must begin with the first step.”

~ Lao Tzu

39. "Your treasure house is in yourself;
It contains all you need."
~ Hui Hai

40. "If you light a lamp for somebody,
It will also brighten your own path."
~ Buddhist Saying

41. "We are shaped by our thoughts;
We become what we think.
When the mind is pure,
Joy follows like a shadow that never leaves."
~ The Buddha

42. "It takes a wise man to learn from his mistakes, but an even wiser one to learn from others."
~ Zen Proverb

43. "The Supreme good is like water
Which nourishes all things without trying to."
~ Lao Tzu

44. "Softness triumphs over hardness,
Feebleness over strength.
What is more malleable is
always superior over that
which is immovable."
~ Lao Tzu

45. "Until he has unconditional
and unbiased love
for all things,
man will not find peace."
~ The Buddha

46. “The disciplined man masters
thoughts by stillness,
and emotions by calmness.”
~ Lao Tzu

47. “Mankind's role is to fulfill his heaven-sent purpose
through a sincere heart that is in harmony with all creation
and loves all things.”
~ Morihei Ueshiba

48. “Lose everything, even the attachment to holiness,
so that you aim only at one thing:
to love.”
~ Chiara Lubich

49. “Your true character is measured
by how you treat those who can do nothing for you.”
~ St. Teresa of Calcutta

50. “Life is an opportunity; benefit from it.
Life is beauty; admire it
Life is a dream; realize it.
Life is a challenge; meet it.
Life is a duty; complete it
Life is a game; play it
Life is a promise; fulfill it
Life is sorrow; overcome it
Life is a song; sing it
Life is a struggle; accept it
Life is a tragedy; confront it
Life is an adventure; dare it
Life is luck; make it
Life is too precious: do not destroy it
Life is life; fight for it.”
~ St. Teresa of Calcutta

51. “The good you do today may be forgotten tomorrow;
Do good anyway.
Give the world the best you have,
and it may never be enough;
Give your best anyway.
For you see, in the end,
it is between you and God;
it was never between you and them, anyway.”
~ St. Teresa of Calcutta

52. “As a single slab of rock
won't budge in the wind,
so, the wise are not moved
by praise, by blame.”
~ The Buddha

My friend, this promise I will afford you. Assimilate, but a few of these beautiful sayings into your being, and they will help guide you to be all that you can be, achieving a higher state of consciousness and spiritual awareness.

Chapter Eleven

Emotional/Mental Plane

How emotionally fit are you? As I explained earlier, our emotions play a huge role in health and disease; they are an outward manifestation of our feelings (energy in motion, if you will), eventually having an impact on your state of mind. Therefore, they should be looked at, faced, forgiven, and, if necessary, healed. We all have emotional baggage we've been carrying around for most of our lives. You may have feelings of fear, worry, or anxiety holding you back from being all you can be.

According to Dr. Sigmund Freud, the world-renowned Australian neurologist and the Father of Psychoanalysis, everything is recorded in the subconscious mind. He explains that you may not consciously remember the details of everything, but deep inside your subconscious, every detail of your life is recorded, which influences your behavior and experiences, even though you are unaware of these underlying influences. Dr. Freud further states that "the subconscious mind can have repressed feelings, hidden memories, habits, thoughts, desires, and reactions." Taking his profound, groundbreaking research and insight into consideration, it seems the most logical way to address someone's emotional and mental state would be to find a way to access the subconscious and reprogram it.

Fortunately, this can be done through positive affirmations. In his insightful book, *Working with Affirmations*, Nayaswami Savitri actually explains, "Affirmations are not just wishful thinking, but practical and dynamic. One reason they work is that they are based on higher truths, which perhaps, we have yet to realize on a conscious level." Swami Kriyananda, in his book, *Affirmations for Self-Healing*, explains affirmations quite eloquently. He states, "An affirmation is a statement of truth which one aspires to absorb into his life, and the greatest mistake people make is to belittle their power to change themselves." Finally, Remez Sasson, a self-improvement writer, states in his book, *The Power of Affirmations*,

"The repetition and corresponding images formed when saying affirmations help them to change the subconscious mind." Dr. Freud once explained thoughts in this way, "Your thoughts come, stay for a while, and then dissipate, allowing new thoughts to enter your mind. Some thoughts stay considerably longer, gaining power and thus affecting your life. They are eventually accepted as real by the subconscious mind since it cannot differentiate reality from what is imagined."

Again, affirmations are a powerful way to incorporate messages into your consciousness. They are positive statements that can help change and, yes, overcome self-sabotaging negative thoughts. At the risk of sounding redundant, understand that with frequent repetition and belief of an affirmation, positive changes in your feelings, as well as your emotions and behavior, can become a reality.

There is an affirmation I would like to share with you that is very powerful. It is called *The Script.* It was created by a hypnotherapist named Carolyn Lybbert after praying for guidance and direction on how to help her clients better help themselves. This powerful tool helped many of her clients become more accountable and responsible individuals who no longer needed to lean on her. *Karol Truman quoted the Script* in her book, *Feelings Buried Alive Never Die* because it had such a powerful impact on her life. If you feel uncomfortable with any of the terminology, Carolyn, its author, says to feel free to substitute any of the words in this affirmation.

The Script

In the name of Jesus Christ...Spirit, Super-Conscious, Subconscious, Conscious, Higher Self, Mind, Will, Nervous System-Brain, Original Intelligence, RNA, DNA, and every genetic anomaly out of alignment with my pattern of perfection, please locate the origin of my conscious and subconscious destructive cellular memories which caused their incorrect perceptions that created/thoughts/beliefs of

(Insert here your feelings/thoughts/beliefs)

Take each and every level, layer, area, and aspect of my Being to these origins. Analyze and resolve them perfectly with God the Father's truth.

Come forward through all generations of time and eternity, healing every event and its appendage based on the origins. Please do it according to God the Father's will, until I'm at the present—filled with light and truth, God's Immanence, peace and love, benevolence, forgiveness of myself for my imperfect perceptions, having compassion for every person, place, circumstance, and event which contributed to any of these destructive cellular memories, feelings, thoughts, or beliefs.

With total forgiveness and unconditional love, I ask that my physical, mental, emotional, and spiritual memory of perfection resonate throughout my Being.

I choose being ____________________(insert positive feeling/etc)
I feel ____________________ (same truth) ________________
I am ____________________ (same truth) ________________

(Replace previous feelings/thoughts/belief with the same desired truth on each line)

It is done! It is healed! It is accomplished now!

Thank you all for coming to my aid and working together to help me rid my Being of stress and attain the full measure of my creation. Thank you, thank you, thank you! I love you and praise you, God the Father, from whom all blessings flow.

Now all facets of my Being, please put this Scripting on automatic, so it repeats itself throughout each and every cell and fiber of my Being every half hour of every day for the next 180 days (or however long is best for me), thereby restoring perfectly healthy frequencies throughout my Being and returning me to my original purpose, power, and magnificence! And it is done!

Please realize that it is essential that you mean what you say and say what you mean when you replace the negative with the positive, for the effectiveness of your processing, will be in direct proportion to the sincerity and intent of your heart.

In addition, I highly recommend the book *Feelings Buried Alive Never Die* by Karol Truman, which deals with how to address feelings and emotions. Chapter 17 gives a list of literally hundreds of negative feelings and their positive opposites that can be inserted into The Script affirmation, some of which may fit your personal needs. Also, Chapter 18 contains an in-depth section on health problems and their probable emotional causes. The information presented in these two chapters and their application to this affirmation can serve as a real springboard to become the best you can be.

Last but not least, I would be remiss if I did not mention a book written by Louise Hay, *I Can Do It*. Discussing topics such as health, forgiveness, prosperity, creativity, relationships, job success, and self-esteem, it shows how you can change virtually every aspect of your life by understanding and using affirmations correctly. She is also the author of the *New York Times* best-selling book. *You Can Change Your Life,* which I also highly recommend to the serious reader looking to take full responsibility for his/her health on an emotional and spiritual level.

In this book, Louise also discusses a technique I recommend to anyone working on positive affirmations. She refers to this technique as "Mirror Work."

"Mirror work is simple and very powerful. It simply involves looking in the mirror when you say your affirmations. Mirrors reflect our true feelings. As children, we received most of our negative messages from adults, many of them looking us straight in the eye and perhaps even shaking a finger at us. Today, when most of us look into a mirror, we'll say something negative. We either criticize our looks or berate ourselves for something else.

To look yourself in the eye and make a positive declaration is one of the quickest ways to get a positive result with affirmations."

She also states, "I also ask people to look in their eyes and say something positive about themselves every time they pass a mirror." Trust me; this is a very powerful technique if employed exactly as she suggests.

Chapter Twelve

Biochemical Plane

Okay, now let's talk about diet and nutrition, which can profoundly affect your biochemistry and, in turn, your health. Remember, food is your best medicine. Granted, nutrition is a very nebulous topic and can be quite confusing to someone trying to take responsibility for his/her health by following a healthy diet. For example, a person can read a book on the health benefits of being a vegetarian and how a meat-based diet can be deleterious to your health, only to follow up with reading about the benefits of being a carnivore like our hunter-gatherer ancestors. Surprisingly enough, there are enough beneficial similarities in both approaches to dieting that you can focus on, although one course might resonate more with you than the other due to your biochemical individuality; there are general rules you can follow for either persuasion and still have a healthy diet.

For the benefit of readers who may not be familiar with the concept of biochemical individuality, it is a term coined by the late renowned biochemist Dr. Roger Williams, Ph.D., in his 1956 groundbreaking book, *Biochemical Individuality–The Basis for the Genetotrophic Concept*. In his book, he explains how we each have unique biochemical traits that determine who we are and how we interact with the world around us. In other words, there is a physiological basis for your psychological makeup. In addition, there are definite rules you should abide by regardless of what type of diet you pursue. The following are a couple dozen "Do's and Don'ts" or general rules that can be applied to any diet you choose:

1. Avoid processed foods such as white flour and white sugar, void of any nutritional value. They cause havoc with your blood sugar levels predisposing you to serious degenerative diseases such as diabetes. The manufacturer is the only one benefitting due to this increasing the shelf life and reducing the spoilage of these products through toxic chemical preservatives, thus improving their bottom line.

2. In general, try to avoid the middle aisles in a supermarket, which usually contain mostly boxed foods that, more often than not, have chemicals added.

3. Read the labels. If you cannot pronounce the words, chances are the food contains chemicals.

4. Make about three-quarters of your meals with as many different colored vegetables as possible. According to Traditional Chinese Medicine, different colors resonate with specific bodily organs (probably due to similar frequencies, wavelengths, and vibrations). For example, red vegetables are good for your heart, black is good for your kidneys, white for your lungs, yellow for your stomach/spleen, and green for your liver.

5. The protein portion of your meal should be no more than the size of your fist to reduce the needed secretion of digestive enzymes so vital to your health. Enzymes break down proteins. They are necessary to keep you alive. If all your enzymes are used for digestion, it will diminish their ability to help with other bodily functions, for example, anti-inflammatory functions.

6. Drink half your body weight in ounces of water daily (i.e., if you weigh 150 lbs., drink at least 75 ounces of water a day). Remember, water is essential for the body to maintain all its essential bodily functions at an optimal level.

7. When possible, avoid drinking bottled water. The longer bottles have been sitting in a facility, possibly being exposed to sunlight, the greater the chance of chemicals being chelated (clawed) from the plastic and into the water.

8. Many people have issues with the gluten found in wheat products, which is ubiquitous and difficult to avoid. It is hard to digest and can cause serious digestive issues. Try to avoid it, and substitute with quinoa or black rice, which are gluten-free. Grains were introduced into our diets about 10,000 years ago, and, consequently, our genetic coding has not yet adapted to this

relatively new change in our diet.

9. Eat your fruits separately between meals. They digest much faster than other macronutrients like protein, fats, and carbohydrates, so, consequently, eating the fruits with your main meals can cause gastric distress such as gas and bloat.

10. Try to avoid or at least cut down on putting ice in your drinks during meals since ice slows down your digestion, causing digestive discomfort.

11. Drink six to eight ounces of water with your meals to assist with digestion via hydrolysis (food breakdown). Conversely, drinking too much at meals can dilute your digestive enzymes, which are vital for good digestion.

12. Avoid vegetable oils—they are pro-inflammatory, being very high in omega-6 fatty acids.

13. Use only cold-pressed extra virgin olive oil for salads and coconut oil for cooking since it tolerates higher heat temperatures.

14. Eat fats high in omega-3 fatty acids (i.e., butter, eggs, salmon, and sardines). Sardines are also high in RNA, which is very good for your memory.

15. Avoid dairy as much as possible since it causes plaque buildup in arteries. One study on over 21,000 males revealed that those who consumed more than two-and-a-half servings of dairy products daily were more likely to develop prostate cancer.

16. Avoid Soy, unless fermented. This includes Soy milk or any other foods processed with Soy. Soy is high in phytoestrogens that act like the hormone estrogen in your body, causing a hormonal imbalance in the body which could cause a phenomenon known as "estrogen dominance." It is linked to breast cancer, infertility, and fibroids in women and gynecomastia in males (breast swelling).

17. Avoid foods containing high-fructose corn syrup. It can cause

inflammation, which is now known to be a precursor to many degenerative diseases, especially diabetes.

18. Avoid sugar-free products. They contain artificial sweeteners, which have claimed to increase the risk of cancer.

19. Avoid Foods containing MSG (Monosodium glutamate). While MSG is used to enhance taste, it also has neurotoxic properties and is linked to obesity.

20. Try to avoid deep-fried foods or at least eat them very sparingly, such as french fries, baked goods, etc. They contain compounds that are the by-product of a high heat frying process known as Acrylamides (above 212 degrees), classified by the EPA as a possible human carcinogen.

21. Eat grass-fed meat and free-range chicken because conventionally raised meat, fish, and poultry contain hormones and antibiotics.

22. Avoid canned foods. Although some manufacturers are phasing it out, some cans used in the canning process still contain bisphenol A (BPA). This compound has been linked to disrupting the endocrine system.

23. Try listening to some relaxing music during dinner, which can reduce stress levels that can compromise digestion.

24. Variety truly is the spice of life. Try not to be too dogmatic with your diet unless you are dealing with severe food allergies or a serious health challenge. Treat yourself once in a while to cuisines you enjoy, but realize you should avoid such delicacies regularly (on vacations and special occasions, I eat anything that doesn't move). So long as this type of indulgence is the exception and not the rule, it should be fine, so go for it! Life is too short. Enjoy!

25. Finally, I admit, this next rule is a difficult one for yours truly: try to chew every bite of food approximately 32 times before

swallowing. I hope this particular concept is not too difficult to swallow. No pun intended! Seriously, don't feel overwhelmed. I suggest including one of these new concepts at a time, and then, once you feel comfortable enough, try adding another.

Hydrogen Water

If possible, drink hydrogenated water because research shows it is a very strong antioxidant and reduces oxidative stress by elevating antioxidants such as glutathione and has strong anti-inflammatory properties. Hydrogen water can correct DNA damage in the mitochondria, which are the energy factories of the cells. There are companies found on the internet that sell pitchers that can house a hydrogen filter. Most filters will last two to three months for a family of four before needing to be changed. Quite reasonable. Thus, a pitcher and filters for a year would cost about one hundred dollars, which is considerably cheaper than money spent over the course of the year drinking bottled water (not to mention avoiding the possible harmful effects of drinking bottled water). Hydrogen molecules also fight allergies by decreasing the body's inflammatory and oxidative reactions. Long-term use can reduce glucose levels as well as triglycerides. It can improve the brain's cognitive function by having the ability to cross the blood-brain barrier and detoxify brain cells, to name a few more of its benefits.

Intermittent Fasting

Intermittent fasting refers to the concept of consuming all your food during an eight-hour window of time, thus fasting for 16 hours each day. This is not as difficult as it may sound initially (unless you have issues like hypoglycemia, which requires having five to six small meals throughout the day). For example, try not eating in the morning until 11 a.m., and then fasting after 7:00 in the evening. Therefore, half of the fasting time will occur during your sleep. Studies have shown that practicing intermittent fasting can lower your insulin levels which are very pro-inflammatory when elevated, not to mention being the precursor to diabetes. This short fast allows your liver to focus more on detoxification during this time since it does not have to focus on digestion. (We will discuss detoxification next).

Detoxification

In her infinite wisdom, Mother Nature has designed multiple pathways for the body to prevent the buildup of toxins from normal metabolic functions through a process known as detoxification. The main player that orchestrates this process is the liver. It accomplishes this feat through a complex dual-stage breakdown of these toxins, which I will attempt to simplify for your benefit. Toxins, such as saturated fats, alcohol, and paint fumes, have a fatty composition. Unfortunately, these toxins cannot be eliminated by the body in this form and thus are required to be made water-soluble to be excreted from the body, one of the liver's main functions.

First, it converts the toxic substances to highly reactive metabolites in phase one of detoxification. Phase two then converts these reactive metabolites further, eventually making them water-soluble, enabling these toxins to be excreted by the kidneys without damaging the renal (kidney) tubules they travel through as they exit the body in the form of urine. The large intestines, the lungs, the kidneys, and the skin also play an active role in detoxification. Actually, the skin will detox any overflow that cannot be cleared by the other four detoxification organs, which will manifest itself as a dermatological condition due to the excessive toxins being excreted via this pathway.

More people are being seen in doctor's offices today for dermatological conditions than ever before. If you doubt this claim, I suggest you call the office of a Dermatologist for an appointment. A new patient can wait up to six or seven weeks for an appointment. Why is this scenario so common? You would think the bodily organs responsible for detoxification were designed in such a manner to clear any toxins that present themselves and avoid putting this toxic load on the skin. Unfortunately, as mentioned earlier, today, the average person is exposed to approximately 80,000 chemicals found in the foods we eat, the water we drink, the air we breathe, and the metabolic by-products of that "stinking thinking," better known as stress. These stressors cumulatively overburden the organs designed to clear these toxins, which then transfer these excess toxins to the skin.

Thus, it is paramount for you to be more proactive and practice different types of detoxification to reduce the toxic burden on the body. This excess of toxins is the precursor to most diseases. Just as a swamp is a breeding ground for all types of pathogens, so too are the cells in your body that are overburdened with a toxic cellular environment. We blame all our sickness and disease on germs that may be present in many disease processes. Germs are part of the normal life cycle.

Let me explain, plants sustain life by assimilating nutrients from the soil via nitrogen-fixing bacteria; in turn, animals sustain life by eating plants (though some animals are carnivores); and man, in turn, who is also omnivorous, sustains life by ingesting plants and animals. Micro-organisms then perform their normal function, completing this life as mentioned earlier. That is by decomposing the organic matter of these species into inorganic matter, recycling said matter into the ecosystem after their demise (thus, the meaning of "ashes to ashes, dust to dust.")

By the way, this concept is addressed in the heart-warming story, "The Lion King." The father, Mufasa, tries to explain to his son, Simba, about the circle of life. Actually, for the most part, it is lowered body resistance (usually due to cellular toxicity) that predisposes us to sickness and disease.

Why was it when there was a pandemic outbreak like the Black Plague, which took place in the 14th century, long before the advent of proper sanitation and modern medicine, which resulted in the death of 75 to 200 million people succumbing to this deadly plague, there were also some who were exposed but survived? Granted, all those who died were infected with a powerful pathogenic bacterium, *Yersinia pestis*; however, the bacteria only victimized those whose resistance was too weak to adapt to the virulence of this deadly bacteria. Think about it! If the bacteria were truly the sole precipitating cause, there should not have been *any* survivors.

Note: Given the present circumstances of being in the COVID-19 Virus Pandemic, I decided to revisit this discussion as mentioned earlier on the role germs play in the disease process, which I believe proves my point. Let me elaborate. Findings from the latest data concerning this Pandemic revealed that people responded differently to this virus ranging from not getting the virus to getting it with mild symptoms or even no symptoms to unfortunate deaths. It is noted that people with underlying conditions and the elderly are more prone to fall victim to the virus. So, in essence, the health experts are saying what? Well, they are saying that the virus itself is not the only precipitating factor involved in this disease process.

It is the ability of the body to resist this pathogen that will dictate whether or not a person will fall victim to the virus and to what degree. Understand, the degree of the inability of the body to adapt to its external environment (the virus) will dictate what kind of deleterious impact, if any, this virus or any other pathogen will have on the body.

When the cells in the body become overburdened with toxins due to an unhealthy lifestyle, these said toxins cannot be efficiently cleared fast enough via the normal pathways of detoxification, causing the cell's "milieu" to become a breeding ground for disease. This swamp-like cellular environment prevents the organelles inside the cells (i.e., mitochondria, which produce the energy for the cells) from performing their normal, necessary functions, thus lowering their resistance and predisposing them to disease. Unfortunately, this is also taking place today in some of our cities right here in America. There are cities in our great country where there exist homeless people living in very unsanitary conditions, causing these regions to become a breeding ground for rats and diseases due to the toxic environment being created from all the accumulated waste. To me, this is a perfect metaphor to explain this phenomenon.

Some of the signs and symptoms that might be caused by an overabundance of toxins in the body include the following: headaches, fatigue, joint aches and pains, weight gain, hormone imbalance, constipation, bloating, gas, skin problems, food cravings, body odor, and bad breath.

Now that you can appreciate the seriousness of this dilemma of toxicity, it would behoove us to explore how we can detoxify our bodies to prevent any unwanted build-up of toxins. However, for a detoxification program to be of any lasting benefit, a healthier lifestyle, which I have just elaborated on, must be considered to avoid spinning your wheels.

Many detoxification programs are of great benefit; however, I have always favored the time-proven "Liver Flush," mainly because detoxifying the liver also upregulates all the many additional functions of the liver besides detoxification.

Due to its many functions, the liver is, for a good reason, the largest solid organ in your body. All the functions of the liver are necessary for survival. Without it, the tissues in your body would die from lack of nutrients; proper digestion would not be possible.

The liver is the metabolic center of your body. It controls the metabolism of our macronutrients (protein, fats, and carbohydrates) via the Central Nervous System. The hormones insulin and glucagon, produced by the pancreas, are the driving force of this metabolic function of the liver. The liver is responsible for the production of bile, proteins for blood plasma, cholesterol, and glucose storage (sugar). The bile your liver produces helps break down fats in the small intestine and take away waste by stimulating peristalsis for the process of defecation.

Fibrinogen and prothrombin, necessary for blood coagulation, and albumin, essential to keep blood cells at an even hydrated level, are also produced by your liver. The production of cholesterol and other proteins is necessary to help transport necessary fats throughout the body. The liver also helps regulate blood sugar by producing, storing, and distributing glucose depending on your body's needs. Although there are additional functions of the liver, I will not bore you with more of the biochemistry of this important organ. Hopefully, you now understand how necessary it is to keep your liver functioning to its full potential, which annual detoxification of your liver can accomplish via a Liver Flush.

Here is a modified version of the Flush, which is not as demanding as the traditional protocol, which takes a week. I found patients complied much more readily to this shorter version which takes only two days. Plan on being home for the day following the Flush due to its cathartic effect.

Ingredients:

- 4 quarts of organic apple juice
- Virgin olive oil
- 5 organic lemons
- 4 organic oranges
- Phosphoric acid (optional)
- Any organic green vegetables
- Filtered water for the alkaline punch to your preferred taste and also for making an Epsom salt mixture

Procedure:

- Drink one 8 oz. glass of apple juice every two hours for a total of 64 oz. (8 glasses in total)

- Optional but highly recommended: add 10 drops of phosphoric acid to each glass of apple juice (80 drops in total).

Note: A two-ounce bottle of Phosphoric Acid is available online at Progressive Labs. It has been thoroughly tested by the FDA and is recognized as safe.

During these two days, in addition to the apple juice, only consume green vegetables and an alkaline citrus punch (squeeze and combine 4 lemons with 4 oranges into at least 32 oz. of water to make the punch).

At the end of the second day of this protocol, take one Tbs. of Epsom salts in warm water at 7 p.m. and another Tbs. at 9 p.m.

Immediately squeeze a fresh lemon into 4 oz. of cold-pressed Virgin olive oil and refrigerate. Drink the cold mixture and lie on your right side, bringing your right leg up to your chest for approximately 45 minutes before going to sleep.

Optional: There is an acupuncture point in the web of the foot between the first and second toe that can be rubbed for a few minutes, which can stimulate the liver.

Let me now explain the rationale for these specific steps, so you adhere to the protocol in the timely fashion suggested. Apple juice is high in malic acid, which acts as a solvent to break up sludge in the gall bladder (adding the phosphoric acid to the apple juice makes for an even stronger mixture for breaking down any adhesions existing between globules of preformed or formed gall stones in some cases).

The function of the Epsom salts via its high magnesium content is to provide relaxation and dilation of the smooth muscle of the common bile duct, which extends from the gall bladder into the duodenum of the small intestine. This will allow broken-down globules to pass from the gall bladder into the duodenum for excretion.

Suppose you have a history of gall bladder issues. In that case, it will be prudent to get an ultrasound of your gall bladder before considering this protocol to determine if you already have large, formed stones which would be too difficult to pass through your bile duct.

Actually, if you have had issues with your gall bladder, I would suggest temporarily postponing the Liver Flush and first try taking one Tbs. of apple cider vinegar in 8 oz. of organic apple juice first thing in the morning for a couple of months before getting an ultrasound to see if you are a candidate for the Flush. Continue this process until you can eventually do the Flush. Finally, the fats in the olive oil mixed with fresh lemon will cause the gallbladder to contract to expel the sludge into your duodenum via your relaxed, dilated, common bile duct.

The bile can become sludge-like and possibly morph into stones because the bile is constantly filtering toxins from your blood. You know what an air conditioner filter could look like if not changed periodically, right? All clogged up and preventing it from functioning efficiently. Well, the same thing happens when your bile gets too thick. It affects your ability to digest your food properly, namely fats.

Consequently, many people can improve their digestion by doing this Liver Flush. I recommend performing the protocol as mentioned earlier for this Flush at least annually. According to Traditional Chinese Medicine, the liver has its highest energy in the springtime and is the ideal time, although not a prerequisite, to do the Flush.

Also do not be alarmed if you experience nausea after consuming the olive oil/lemon mixture. This is to be expected due to the contraction of the gall bladder in response to the concentrated fat content of this mixture. Have a cup of warm ginger tea already prepared to alleviate the nausea, and prevent regurgitation which will could possibly nullify the Flush.

Now that we have talked about the benefits of detoxification and how to rid the body of toxins, we can soon focus on what to put into this sacred vessel and its benefits to the body in the section on

Superfoods.

Chapter Thirteen

Physical Plane

We all know the benefits of exercise. It improves our circulation of blood which carries oxygen to the body's cells and their mitochondria (energy factories of the cells), eliciting a feeling of well-being.

There are some basic movements that can be performed in the confines of your home that are not too time-consuming nor too difficult to perform yet can be very beneficial to your health.

Stretching: Do you know why it feels so good as you instinctively stretch when you first awaken in the morning? Well, unlike your cardiovascular system, which has a pump (your heart) that constantly moves your blood throughout your body, your lymph system, which is so vital for detoxification of the metabolic waste from your cells, has no such pump to eliminate this accumulated overnight waste into the blood for excretion.

This detoxification process depends solely on body movement. Thus, your body, in its infinite wisdom, instinctively causes you to perform a feel-good stretch, which, in turn, mobilizes the stagnated lymph waste in order to be excreted into the bloodstream and filtered by your kidneys. Stretching can also be accomplished by using a 39-inch foam cylinder. Very economical, one can be purchased at a sporting goods store for about $30. Make sure you buy one that includes a video that demonstrates how to use the cylinder on different muscles. YouTube is filled with inexpensive yoga videos, which are also available to purchase to learn different yoga posture stretches.

Understand that your blood vessels, acupuncture meridians, lymphatic vessels, and nerve fibers travel between the muscles and their protective coverings (known as fascia). Adhesions (a form of scar tissue) can form between these muscles and coverings due to trauma or stress. Exercise, including stretching, Yoga postures (known as asanas), Tai Chi, and Qi Gong, can unblock stuck energy in the body's acupuncture meridians, as well as enhancing the flow of blood and lymph and the conduction of nerve impulses by breaking up adhesions between the coverings of the muscles (fascia) and the actual muscle, via their respective movements and postures. This is why deep fascia massage can be a very therapeutic modality. The application of this type of therapy can break up adhesions between the muscles and their fascia coverings (picture overcooked spaghetti).

Walking is an easy, relaxing form of exercise if you prefer the outdoors. If walking is your preference, do not let inclement weather stop you. Try taking a walk in a mall if convenient. Fifteen to twenty minutes three times a week should suffice.

If physically possible, after walking on a regular basis for a couple of weeks, try some interval speed walking. For example, walk briskly for one minute, then walk normally for a couple of minutes. Do three sets of interval speed walking, which will take nine minutes.

It might be challenging initially, but I promise it will eventually become easier and quite rewarding. Studies have shown it can upregulate your metabolism, which means it increases the body's metabolic response by causing your body to continue burning calories up to as much as 48 hours after this type of walking has been completed. Interval speed walking will also produce more of the feel-good endorphins that will negate the visceral fat-storing hormone cortisol, which, in turn, will help you lose "belly fat" weight if this type of walking is performed on a regular basis.

By the way, recent research now shows that extensive cardio training of 40 minutes to an hour can be a stressor to the body that can increase cortisol levels that lead to the dreaded aforementioned "belly fat" that is harmful to your health. Therefore, if you have been religiously going to the gym for a couple of hours a day a few times a week without noticing any marked fat loss, especially in the mid-section, consider the fact that you are putting too much stress on your body, leading to an increase of cortisol which causes your body to store fat.

Another exercise that can be performed in your home that I have been using for decades is the use of a mini trampoline, also known as a Rebounder (approx. 36-42" in diameter and 7-8" in height). Also available are models with handrails if you have an issue with balance, which will improve in time if used regularly. Studies performed by NASA on the astronauts found many benefits from rebounding, including:

Due to the low impact of rebounding, it is less stressful on the body joints.

Increases bone mass.

Upregulates the flow of lymph by creating a G-Force around the body. G-Force refers to the force created around the body as a result of acceleration or gravity. That is, when you jump on a trampoline initially, you jump upwards, pause for less than a second, at a point where you are weightless, then decelerate, followed by impact and repeat.

Aids in detoxification via draining the lymph system.

Upregulates the immune system by increasing the production of white blood cells.

Upregulates the cardiovascular system by increasing circulation.

Improves balance.

Builds physical strength and muscular development.

Improves proprioception (perception or awareness of the position and movement of the body) for enhancing athletic performance and a sense of general well-being as people age.

It is an efficient way to burn calories for weight loss.

It has also been known to improve varicose veins and reduce cellulitis.

All you have to do is bounce gently on the trampoline. Your feet do not even have to leave the trampoline to receive the benefits of rebounding. To receive all the benefits from rebounding, it is suggested to do 15-20 minutes a day.

Rebounding for 5 minutes 3-4 times a day will provide a longer period of enhanced blood circulation, making for an even healthier cardiovascular system. If someone is vertically challenged, they can also benefit from rebounding by just sitting on it and bouncing up and down without taking the buttocks off the rebounder due to the G-Force phenomenon.

Contra-indications: While it is a fact that exercise, in general, is very beneficial for the heart, Rebounding has an even more beneficial effect due to the G-force it creates from this dynamic exercise by increasing circulation and detoxification.

However, anyone with hypertension or blood pressure over 180/100 should refrain from rebounding since this level is already over-taxing the heart allowing very little rest between beats during its diastolic phase. The diastolic blood pressure is the bottom of the two numbers. With blood pressure at a more suitable level (under (180/100), rebounding can definitely strengthen the heart muscle and improve circulation. It is advised to check with your primary care provider if you have or are predisposed to hypertension.

Chapter Fourteen

Sleep

I have decided to discuss the topic of sleep because of the wide-reaching impact it has on one's health status. While this will not be a "deep dive" into the different stages of sleep and their significant importance where the phenomenon of sleep is concerned (there are many informative books which cover, in detail, this important topic), I will offer some basic information to hopefully help improve your quality and quantity of this essential bodily function. You see, from a holistic perspective, regardless of how dedicated you are towards a healthy lifestyle, unless you experience good quality sleep, you will, unfortunately, fail to achieve your goal of a balanced state of health, which will eventually optimize your quality and quantity of life.

Let me elaborate. You may have a very healthy lifestyle, which includes employing a healthy organic diet; an ideal amount of exercise, which avoids elevation of the stress hormone Cortisol, which can have a deleterious effect on the body; have an attitude of gratitude and being the first to love by serving others; perform meaningful positive affirmations to reprogram your subconscious; and being mindful of meaningful, constructive concepts where your emotions are concerned (i.e., being patient in one moment of anger you will escape a hundred days of sorrow); but do not have good sleep habits, you will not experience the desired balanced state of health to which we have been referring.

Therefore, I feel it is incumbent upon me to discuss the phenomenon of sleep and how to address it from a holistic perspective to reach the desired outcome of possibly overcoming and preventing sleep deprivation. Most experts agree that at least 10 percent of the United States population suffers from this debilitating condition.

Before addressing how to improve one's sleep, let's discuss some of the reasons why a "good night's sleep" is so critical to your health. In general, your brain utilizes sleep time for restoration to maintain proper homeostasis by checking all bodily systems for any imbalances, thus enabling you to adapt to your internal and external environment. This is why infants and young children require more sleep than adults.

In her infinite wisdom, Mother Nature realizes that due to their required increased metabolism to optimize growth, they consequently require more sleep to allow extra time for rebalancing of all the body systems due to the increased demand being placed on it.

To induce sleep, your body produces a hormone called melatonin. Once darkness occurs, a tiny gland located between the two cerebral hemispheres of the brain, the pineal gland, secretes melatonin. This is why we sleep when it is dark and wake up when it gets light – daylight turns off the production of melatonin.

The average recommended sleep time is between seven to nine hours, depending on your individual needs. Reduced melatonin levels can be observed in various disease states, such as mood disorders, dementia, cancer, severe pain, as well as Type 2 Diabetes. The reduction can also be due to deviations and disruptions of normal body circadian rhythms (a phenomenon prevalent in rotating shift work), which I will explain shortly. In addition, studies have shown how the pineal gland, as mentioned earlier, is likely to sense Low Electromagnetic Frequencies as light, which can lead to a disruption and reduction of melatonin levels. Research by the International Agency for Research on

Cancer (IARC) classifies EMFs as possibly being carcinogenic to human beings since they might transform normal cells into cancer cells. So, from where do these Extremely Low EMFs (EL-EMFs) come? Sources include power lines, electrical wiring, electrical appliances such as shavers, alarm clocks, hairdryers, and electric blankets, radio waves, microwaves, Wi-Fi routers, phones, and television sets, just to name a few. To reduce EMFs when using your cell phone, go to your phone's settings for display and brightness to shut off your phone's blue light. The screen will have an amber hue, but that means less exposure to EMFs.

Even Fitbit watches, which are popularly being worn to monitor your sleep patterns, can negatively affect the quality of deep sleep.

Therefore, I strongly suggest turning off the circuit breaker in your bedroom when it is time to fall asleep. The mechanism by which these low frequencies may be harmful is that they disrupt the low current naturally emitted by your body and overheat the cells (the human body vibrates at approximately 5-10 Hz). Also, there are many companies that offer shielding devices and even clothing to block low EMFs (in China, pregnant women wear special clothing to block low EMFs to protect their unborn). You can go online and Google "low EMF shielding devices" and check it out if this topic is of interest to you.

Unfortunately, just turning off the circuit breaker to your bedroom may not be enough to avoid sleeping problems. However, since these frequencies are potentially hazardous to your health (it is bad enough that you are bombarded every day during your activities of daily living from these EL-EMFs), it should definitely be considered. The main cause for some people may be a physical obstruction blocking their air passage, thus reducing one's airflow (oxygen reduction), known as Sleep Apnea. For example, someone may have a deviated nasal septum or a large tongue occupying too much space in the mouth, or even an enlarged uvula (a teardrop-shaped tissue hanging down the back of the throat that helps produce saliva and prevent food and liquids from going up your nose when you eat), being overweight, or even structural misalignments of the jaw, commonly known as TMJ (Temporomandibular-joint), and spinal column known as vertebral subluxation (both of these conditions will be discussed shortly).

Since I believe being overweight is the most common obstructive offender, let me explain how it can obstruct the air passages in the body. Excess body fat can hide in places that cannot be observed by the naked eye, including along the airways and beneath the tongue.

This crowding, in combination with added weight pressing from the outside such as increased neck size or an enlarged stomach reducing lung volumes, collapses the airways and causes problems, which can all lead to disrupted breathing, causing snoring and sleep apnea which can diminish airflow to the lungs and then the brain (hypoxia). This can be very serious since brain cells are very sensitive to oxygen deprivation and can begin to die within five minutes after their oxygen supply has been cut off. Longer periods can cause coma, seizures, and even brain death.

To combat this problem, patients suffering from sleep apnea are first given a device to wear during sleep to monitor their oxygen intake to determine if they are candidates for a CPAP machine (continuous positive airway pressure machine). Another alternative which can be helpful, depending on the cause of the airway blockage, is a tailor-made night guard designed by a skilled dentist called a TMJ appliance to move the jaw forward, and consequently, the tongue as well if the tongue is enlarged and causing obstruction of the air passage. (This is an important joint in the body that connects the upper and lower jaws. It can become misaligned from a trauma very easily because of its hinge-like anatomy, causing painful symptoms such as headaches, tinnitus (ringing in the ears), earaches, and pain behind the eyes, which eventually lead to insomnia due to the severity of the pain).

Finally, in the previously mentioned vertebral subluxation condition, a misaligned vertebra "pinches" nerves exiting from the spinal column. Understand, the nervous system acts as a communication center between the brain and the body due to its ability to transmit energy impulses conducted along its pathways. The pressure on the nerve root exiting the spinal column due to the misaligned vertebrae interferes with this communication between the brain and the body tissues, causing them to malfunction,

Therefore, without getting too technical, you can have a scenario in which there is a misalignment of the first vertebrae of the spinal column, located at the base of the skull, causes pressure on the brain stem. This can decrease the necessary blood flow to the brain. Since a normal blood supply is essential for the required uptake of oxygen to the brain, any decrease of this vital nutrient can disrupt the sleep cycle due to the lack of oxygen to the brain, causing sleep deprivation

A good analogy would be a damaged sprinkler system resulting in "brown spots" on the lawn due to the diminished water supply. If vertebral subluxation is, in fact, the main cause of sleep deprivation, a skilled doctor of Chiropractic would be the professional to consult to correct this condition".

Obviously, the cause of the airway obstruction will dictate which attempted fix may or may not help. Besides those already mentioned, additional factors can also contribute to sleep problems that might have to be addressed to improve one's sleep patterns. To be more specific, I am referring to a poor lifestyle. Let me elucidate if you will:

1. **Not having the ideal temperature for sleep**
   In general, the suggested temperature in the bedroom should be between 60- and 67-degrees F. to optimize quality sleep time. You see, while lying in bed to go to sleep, your metabolism slows down, and your body temperature decreases to induce sleep. The aforementioned suggested temperature can help speed up the process.

2. **Leaving a night light on**
   This can cause the light-sensitive pineal gland to secrete less of the all-important hormone melatonin, as explained previously, so try to sleep in total darkness.

3. **Eating refined carbs (Sugar) right before bedtime**
   This should be avoided. Ingesting sugar may initially elevate your blood sugar and cause a hypoglycemic (low blood sugar) response in the long run by overstimulating the organs responsible for regulating blood sugar. Namely the pancreas and liver. Like a car going downhill with no brakes, these overly excited organs remove more sugar from the blood than was ingested before they calm down, leading to low blood sugar, which can cause your brain to wake you up since low glucose levels (sugar) will cause the body to produce cortisol and adrenalin which will cause the previously discussed "fight or flight" stress phenomenon. This undesirable hormonal response not only will wake you up but make it very difficult to go back to sleep.

4. **Having stimulants such as caffeine and alcohol prior to bedtime**
   This has the same effect as sugar on your endocrine system (elevated cortisol and adrenaline), with the same undesired result – sleeplessness.

5. **Watching a movie that causes an emotional response such as fear, anxiety, or sadness late at night.**
   This can also have a negative impact on the body, similar to points three and four, where body hormones are affected.

6. **Discussing problems that must be addressed with your significant other prior to bedtime**
   This should also be put off until daytime to avoid a hormonal response. This may sound ridiculous to some, but hopefully, you are starting to realize how your mind can impact your physiology, for better or worse.

7. **Irregular bedtime schedule**
   This causes a disruption of the body's natural rhythm. Your body goes through a wake-sleep cycle known as the circadian rhythm, which helps keep you awake during the day and asleep during the night. Thus, going to sleep at different times causes confusion with this cycle which, in this state, makes it difficult for your body to adjust to sleeping or waking. Consequently, you may feel sleeplessness at night and sleepiness during the day.

8. **Medications**
   Some medications that can cause sleep disturbance are corticosteroids, alpha-blockers, statins, ACE inhibitors, SSRI antidepressants, glucosamine, and cholinesterase inhibitors. These are the most common drugs that can have

a negative impact on your sleep. However, other medications may also affect your sleep, so if you are on any medication and are experiencing difficulty sleeping, discuss it with your doctor to see if your medication might be the culprit.

9. **Allergies**

   Hypersensitive people prone to allergies may experience irritated airways, making it difficult to breathe if exposed to allergens. This can make it hard to fall asleep or cause a person to wake up, similar to someone suffering from sleep apnea.

A "Bakers Dozen" of the Most Common Signs and Symptoms of a Sleep Disorder

If you struggle with sleep and experience any of the following symptoms, you may want to consider visiting your doctor to be tested for a sleep disorder:

Difficulty falling asleep

Waking up too early

Not feeling refreshed upon waking up

Inability to sleep through the night

Fatigue and low energy during the day

Waking up with chest pains or shortness of breath

Loud snoring

Restless leg syndrome. An uncomfortable sensation and an urge to move your legs while you try to fall asleep

Difficulty concentrating

Mood disturbances such as irritability

Behavioral problems such as aggression or feeling impulsive

Difficulty with relationships including family, friends, and caregivers

Difficulty at work or school

Suggestive "Old Folk Medicine" Sleep Aids for Sleep Support

Most people dislike the idea of having to take medicine to fall asleep because it can be habit-forming and also dangerous.

Therefore, if you do not have any physical airway obstructions, which may require a CPAP machine, a TMJ appliance, a vertebral misalignment, or do not have any issues with being markedly overweight, here are some natural remedies to try if you are having sleep issues:

1. **Aromatherapy** – Add some essential oils to water, namely lavender, rose, or lemon oil, to name a few, to a diffuser next to your nightstand. The vapors being inhaled are very calming to the body and will help induce sleep.

2. **Have a cup of tea** comprised of certain herbs, namely chamomile, hops, passion flow, sage, fresh ginger, or valerian root (nasty taste but quite effective, being one of the main ingredients in the drug Valium).

3. **Nutmeg** can be a sedative. Steep half a crushed nutmeg in hot water for 10 minutes and drink it a half-hour before bedtime.

4. **A relaxing bath** – Have that cup of one of the sleep-inducing teas I just suggested prepared to drink as soon as you get out of the tub. Add a combination of a few drops of lavender, passionflower, or rosemary oil to your warm bath. By the time you finish your bath and have your cup of tea, you should feel wound down and ready to doze off.

5. **A glass of elderberry** at room temperature can be a sleep inducer. You can get pure elderberry concentrate at your local health food store. Just dilute it to your taste, drink it, and" hit the hay."

6. **Hop Pillow.** According to legend, King George III of England (1738-1820) was plagued with insomnia until a physician prescribed a hop pillow. Hops have been known to have a

tranquilizing effect, as mentioned earlier. Lupulin, an active ingredient in hops, has been used to treat a variety of nervous disorders. So, if the spirit moves you, buy or sew together a little fine white cotton bag. Fill the bag with hops and tack it onto your pillow. Change the hops once a month. (Note: it is believed that the hop pillow will be a more effective sedative if you lightly spray it with rubbing alcohol)

7. Eating a large salad with only a little olive oil and sea salt. Lettuce contains lactucarium, a calming agent. Unfortunately, lettuce is also a diuretic. Therefore, if this is something you might like to try, don't go overboard with the lettuce, or you might find yourself having to go to the bathroom in the middle of the night, which kind of defeats its purpose. Galen, a Greek physician, writer, and philosopher (129-216 AD), was able to cure his insomnia by eating lots of lettuce in the evening.

8. Flaxseed eye pillow. Placing an eye pillow filled with flax seed over the eyes may help you fall asleep. They can be purchased at most health food stores.

9. Goat's milk. Some naturopathic doctors recommend drinking 6 ounces of goat's milk (it contains a high level of calcium and tryptophan, which are very calming to the body) before each meal and 6 ounces before bedtime. Most health food stores carry goat's milk. (Caution, if you are on certain medications (psychotropic drugs), too much tryptophan can be contra-indicated, so check with your physician first.)

10. Slow Deep Breathing. Deep breathing has a profound relaxing effect on your autonomic nervous system, which can induce sleep. There are many good techniques, and here is a simple one that I like. It is a variation of an ancient yoga technique (Bhramari pranayama breathing exercises) developed by Dr. Andrew Weil. It helps people relax as it replenishes oxygen to the body.

These steps will help you follow the breathing as mentioned earlier exercise:

1. Close your eyes and breathe deeply in and out.
2. Cover your ears with your hands.
3. Place your index fingers one each above your eyebrows and the rest of your fingers over the eyes.
4. Next, put gentle pressure on the sides of your nose and focus on your brow area.
5. Keep your mouth closed and breathe out slowly through your nose, making the humming "OM" sound.
6. Repeat the process five times.

Note: In clinical studies, this type of yogic breathing has been shown to quickly reduce the breathing and heart rate, which tends to be very calming and can prepare your body for sleep.

At the beginning of this chapter, I explained why taking responsibility for your health by incorporating a healthy, holistic lifestyle in your activities of daily living may be an exercise in futility, where your goal of optimum health is concerned, if you do not get at least 7-9 hours of sleep each night. Actually, even sleeping that many hours still may not constitute a "good night's sleep." It is the *quality* of your sleep that will determine an ideal sleep response.

Let me explain. It is imperative that you achieve the state of deep sleep for your body to enter into a restorative stage of repair and regeneration of new tissues, build bones and muscles, and even strengthen the immune system. People 30 years of age get about two hours of deep sleep a night, while those over 65 might only get 30 minutes. This also is the stage where your body produces HGH (human growth hormone), commonly referred to as the "fountain of youth" hormone. It regulates body composition, body fluids, muscle and bone growth, mental function, and possibly heart function, thus having a far-reaching positive impact on body performance. Unfortunately, older adults do not secrete as much HGH as younger people since they have a shortened deep stage of sleep, as mentioned earlier.

While some people get HGH injections to upregulate their levels, they must have their blood levels checked at least every six months to avoid a hormone imbalance that can have serious side effects (e.g., cancer).

It can also be very costly, ranging from $1500 to $2000 monthly. A more conservative way to upregulate HGH production would be to increase the amount of time spent in the stage of deep sleep. Most experts agree that 75% of HGH is produced during the deep sleep stage. Research has shown that certain nutrients taken at bedtime may positively affect upregulating the deep sleep stage.

Here are some researched nutrients which have been shown to accomplish this objective:

1. Ashwagandha - (known as the King of Herbs) is used in the traditional Hindu system of medicine. Studies have shown that this Ayurvedic, anti-stress herb gets you to sleep faster and puts you into a deeper sleep faster.

2. Theanine - an amino acid found in both green and black tea leaves and certain mushrooms (Bay Bolete). It promotes relaxation without drowsiness. Caution: May lower blood pressure. Avoid if you already have low blood pressure, if pregnant, or breastfeeding. Children from 8 thru 12 can take up to 200 mg. twice daily for up to five months.

3. Melatonin - as mentioned earlier, a hormone produced by the light-sensitive pineal gland, which puts you into a deeper sleep and increases the spikes of HGH eight-fold, according to research.

4. Tryptophan - an essential amino acid with the same effect as melatonin on deep sleep and HGH. Warning: Be sure to consult your doctor first if you take any mood-enhancing or psychotropic medication.

5. L-Arginine - a semi-essential amino acid (unable to be synthesized by preterm infants) can promote relaxation and sleep. Caution: if someone has a history of cold sores or genital herpes, too much in the system can potentially trigger the virus that causes those conditions. It can also exacerbate allergies or asthma, so caution should be taken by anyone suffering from these conditions by consulting with an alternative doctor.

6. Lysine - An essential amino acid that has been shown to reduce anxiety. Caution: high dosage can lead to diarrhea, abdominal pain, kidney inflammation, and possibly kidney failure. Consult with an alternative doctor for your specific dosage if considering taking this amino acid for relaxation.

7. Magnesium - research indicates supplemental Magnesium can improve sleep quality, especially in people with poor sleep.

Magnesium can also help insomnia that is linked to the sleep disorder Restless Leg Syndrome. It also reduces stress and stabilizes mood. Finally, Magnesium increases the neurotransmitter GABA, which encourages relaxation as well as sleep.

While these nutrients are markedly cheaper than HGH injections, they could still be pretty costly. My advice would be to do some homework. Some manufacturers can be searched out on the internet with a product that includes most, if not all, of the ingredients as mentioned earlier.

There is a good book written by Dr. Arlene K. Unger, *Sleep*, which has some nice exercises and affirmations to facilitate your getting a good night's sleep. It is a small size that can be kept on your nightstand for quick reference when preparing to go to sleep.

Also, don't be surprised if that stubborn belly fat starts melting away once your deep sleep issue is finally being addressed and corrected.

According to Dr. Michael Breus, PhD, author of *Beauty Sleep*, studies have shown that your metabolism will not function properly if you are not getting enough minutes of good quality sleep (deep sleep) each day. Evidently, lack of deep sleep slows down your metabolism. It decreases the hormone Leptin (made by your fat cells), which decreases appetite and spikes the hormone Ghrelin, increasing appetite, which can also play a role in difficulty losing weight. Therefore, if you have tried and adhered to every possible diet with no satisfactory outcome, a lack of deep sleep might be the culprit.

This concludes my discussion on the importance of sleep, the possible causes of sleep deprivation, and suggestions to address such issues. Hopefully, this will afford the reader a more penetrating insight into the phenomenon of sleep and how to enhance it.

Chapter Fifteen

Essential Oils

Essential oils are made by distilling tree bark, flowers, fruit leaves, seeds, or roots. These oils protect plants and trees from insects. Since they are composed of very tiny molecules, they can enter the body's cells and have a therapeutic effect. The oils derived from vegetables and nuts possess much larger molecules and cannot penetrate the bi-lipid layer of the cell wall. Thus they cannot have a therapeutic effect like essential oils.

The first known civilization to use essential oils were the Egyptians, dating as far back as 4500 BC. They were renowned for their knowledge in the application of aromatic oils and ointments for cosmetic and medicinal purposes. We will discuss some of the more important ones and their unique effect on the body, as suggested by Dr. Josh Axe, a brilliant, well-known chiropractor, and nutritionist.

Frankincense: I mention this oil first because it is generally regarded as the king of essential oils because of its many medicinal uses. It comes from distilling the resin from the Boswellia tree. It was considered a very special gift in biblical times, named more often than any other essential oil in the Bible. It was one of the gifts of the Magi (the Three Wise Men) when they visited Christ at His birth.

It can be applied in several ways. When applied topically, it can help heal bruises due to trauma and reduce joint pain due to its anti-inflammatory properties. It is also good for age spots and scars (mix a few drops with some organic moisturizing cream). If taken internally, only use 2-3 drops mixed in water. It is said to shrink tumors and help with dementia and tics due to its ability to cross the difficult blood-brain barrier. When inhaled by using a diffuser, it can help with respiratory ailments. It is said that when in doubt, use Frankincense.

Lavender: This oil is one of the most widely used essential oils because of its many benefits; it is great for anxiety and stress reduction in general. If you are having difficulty sleeping, put a few drops on the pillowcase or put a few drops in a diffuser to help you sleep. If mixed with a few drops of coconut oil as a carrier, it can also be applied topically to the skin for scrapes, cuts, or skin burns. I can personally testify to its healing properties where burns are concerned. I lost my balance while in a sauna a few years ago. Unfortunately for yours truly, there was no cedar guard around the sauna unit, and I came in direct contact with the unit, causing a very serious second-degree burn. When first seen for medical attention, I was told it was a borderline third-degree burn, possibly requiring a skin graft. Well, to cut to the chase, I made a poultice of lavender oil, chlorophyll powder, Aloe Vera, vitamin E, and Manuka honey. I applied it twice daily for a couple of weeks, leaving no residual scarring. My doctors were amazed!

Oregano oil: One of my favorites when in clinical practice, this very potent oil should only be used for no more than a week straight using a few drops in water. It has strong anti-bacterial, anti-fungal, anti-viral, and anti-parasitic properties and is great for Candidiasis (yeast overgrowth in the gut). It is also good for gingivitis and bad breath and Coryza (Irritation and swelling of the mucous membrane in the nose caused by the common cold or allergies).

Myrrh (holy anointing oil): Myrrh also has many healing properties. It is a known antiseptic and is said to improve mood and balance hormones. It is good for bacterial, fungal, and parasitic infections. It can be mixed with frankincense in a diffuser to enhance meditation or tea tree oil for skin infection. Also, it can be applied topically to gums for toothaches.

Peppermint oil: Well known as a remedy for bad digestion and bad breath, peppermint oil also has many other therapeutic qualities. It can be used as a mouthwash, is good for enhancing the ability to focus, and improves memory. Taking three deep breaths of this amazing oil is a great pick-me-up if tired. Also, you can put a drop of peppermint in water for a better workout or exercise. It can be applied to stiff muscles and is also good for bloating, gas, and nausea – mix a couple of drops with coconut oil. It's good for fever and can be mixed with lavender oil and rubbed on the temples for headaches (a few drops each). This mixture is also good for sunburn.

Tea tree oil: This great antiseptic is very gentle on the skin. It's good for psoriasis and eczema when combined with lavender oil and is also good for dandruff when mixed with lemon oil (approximately 20 drops each). It is good for acne when mixed with Manuka honey (leave on the area for about five minutes). Due to anti-fungal properties, it can help with athlete's foot. It also kills mold when mixed with oregano oil.

Bergamot: This oil is often used in colognes and perfumes. It is good for reducing the symptoms of depression; just put a few drops in a diffuser or carry a bottle with you to inhale if prone to moodiness. It is good for the digestive system and upregulates the immune system. If congested with phlegm and mucus, simply add a couple of drops in water and swallow. It can also be mixed with mint and rosemary to make a shampoo.

Cedar oil (Cedarwood oil): Cedar oil, derived from conifer trees mostly in the pine and cypress families, is known to help Attention Deficit Disorder when diffused. It is good for skin conditions such as eczema and psoriasis when applied topically and also can be used as a deodorant. It is also said to thicken hair by growing new follicles when mixed with aloe vera and rosemary. Although some essential oils are safe to take orally in minimal amounts, Cedarwood oil or Cedar oil should ***not*** be taken internally.

Chapter Sixteen

The Bach Flower Remedies

The Bach Flower Remedies are a safe and natural method of healing discovered by Dr. Edward Bach, an English homeopathic physician who practiced from the 1920s-1930s. He spent his life exploring the use of flowers and plants as a means of promoting emotional well-being. In total, he identified 38 natural remedies, each one derived from a different wildflower, plant, or tree, each corresponding to a different emotional state. They gently restore the balance between mind and body by casting out negative emotions such as worry, fear, hatred, and indecision, to name a few, which interfere with a person's equilibrium as a whole.

These remedies are quite powerful. After being in practice for over ten years, I learned about these remedies and decided to take the classes to incorporate their use in my practice. It is gratifying to note that patients carrying around emotional baggage (the most difficult to help), which quite often contributed to their physical ailments, responded more favorably when these remedies were administered with other lifestyle recommendations.

If you would like to know more about the Bach Flower Remedies, or the Bach Education Program, you can contact Nelsons Solutions by calling 1-978-988-3833 or 1-800-319-9151 or by email at USACustomerService@nelsons.net. Their website is www.Nelsons.net. Nelsons has been administering these wonderful remedies since 1860 and are considered by many to be the authority when it comes to these remedies.

Here are the 38 remedies with their indications:

Source: Nelson's Dilution website: www.NelsonsDilution.com.

Agrimony: For the jovial, humorous, and cheerful people who love peace at any cost to them. These people are willing to agree, though they give up much to avoid being distressed by argument or quarrel. Though these people generally have trouble and are tormented and restless while being worried in their minds and bodies, they hide their cares behind their humor and are considered very good friends to know. They often take drugs or alcohol to stimulate themselves to help bear their trials with cheerfulness.

Key Traits: Addiction, unhappy, anxiety, and insomnia.

Human Indication: Mental torment behind a brave face. Appear care-free and humorous to mask anxieties and unhappiness.

Aspen: For people who have vague and unknown fears for which there is no explanation or reason. There is a terror that something awful is going to happen even though it is unclear what exactly that is. These vague inexplicable fears may haunt by day or night. Sufferers may often be afraid to share their troubles with others.

Key Traits: Fear, worries, unknown fears.

Human Indications: Fears and worries of unknown origin.

Beech: For those who feel the need to see more good and beauty in all that surrounds them. Much appears to be wrong to them, and they do not have the ability to see the beauty within all that surrounds them. Beech enables them to be more tolerant, lenient, and understand the different way each individual and all things are working to their perfection.

Key Traits: Intolerance, critical, lack of compassion.

Human Indication: When you need more tolerance toward other people.

Centaury: Kind, quiet, gentle people who are over-anxious to serve others. They overtax their strength in their endeavors. Their wish so grows upon them that they become more servants than willing helpers. Their good nature leads them to do more than their share of work and, in doing so, may neglect their particular mission in life.

Key Traits: Weak-willed, bullied, unable to say no, imposed upon, timid, lacking energy, tired, passive, quiet.

Human Indication: When you have a hard time saying no, and you get easily imposed upon.

Cerato: Those who have not sufficient confidence in themselves to make their own decisions. They constantly seek advice from others and are often misguided.

Key Traits: Confirmation, seeking advice, do not trust own wisdom or judgment.

Human Indications: When you do not trust your judgment in decision-making.

Cherry Plum: For the fear of one's mind being over-strained and of doing fearful and dreadful things. Unfortunately, these thoughts and impulses continue to arise, causing an uncontrollable desire and impulse to do them anyway.

Key Traits: Fear of losing control, temper tantrums, breakdown, abusive rage, explosive outbursts.

Human Indications: A loss of self-control, including violent outbursts.

Chestnut Bud: For those who do not take advantage of observation and experience and take a longer time than others to learn the early lessons of daily life. Where one experience would be enough for some to "get it," the chestnut type finds it necessary to have more, and even sometimes several experiences, to finally learn the lesson. Therefore, to their regret, they find themselves having to make the same mistake on different occasions when once should have been enough, or observation of others could have saved them, perhaps even that one fault. The expression, "The wiser person learns from others' mistakes," certainly does not apply to this type of individual.

Key Words: Repeating mistakes

Human Indications: Keep repeating the same mistakes. Don't learn from past mistakes.

Chicory: For those who are very aware of the needs of others, they tend to supervise.

They tend to think that they know what is best for these individuals. They are always trying to make things right for them. They are constantly correcting what they consider wrong and doing so with great enjoyment. They desire to be near anyone for whom they care.

Key Words: Possessive, over-protective, self-centered, critical, nagging, self-pitying, easily offended, manipulating, and demanding.

Human Indication: When you find yourself manipulating and controlling your loved ones.

Clematis: For those who are dreamy, drowsy, not fully awake, who have no great interest in life. Quiet people who are not very happy in their present circumstances, living more in the future than in the present, living in the hopes that someday their dreams will come true. When ill, they make little or no effort to get better, perhaps even welcoming death in the hope of meeting once again someone beloved they have lost.

Key Words: Daydreaming, withdrawing, and lack of concentration.

Human Indication: Have a tendency to live in their dream world with little interest in what is going on in the real-world, accident-prone daydreamer.

Crab Apple: This is a cleansing remedy for someone who feels there is something not quite clean about themselves to the point of being obsessive about it, regardless of how insignificant it might be.

Key Words: Poor self-image, sense of not being clean, obsessive.

Human Indication: For those who feel unclean or have a hard time accepting their self-image.

Elm: For those who are trying to follow their calling in life of trying to do something good and of importance for the benefit of humanity. However, at times they may feel depressed and overwhelmed, thinking the task they have undertaken is more than they can handle and, in fact, not within the power of any human being to accomplish.

Key Words: Depression, overwhelmed by responsibilities, despondent, exhausted.

Human Indication: Feeling overwhelmed and depressed, like there is too much to do and that it is impossible to do it all.

Gentian: For those who get easily discouraged. If something causes a small delay or hinders their progress, they tend to get disheartened and give up on anything they were working towards.

Key Words: Discouraged, depressed.

Human Indication: When one gets easily discouraged when facing any difficulty.

Gorse: For those who feel very hopeless that anything can be done to help them. If ill, they may try different treatments but feel all hope is lost for their recovery.

Key Words: Hopelessness, despair, pessimism.

Human Indication: When one has the extreme feeling of hopelessness and despair.

Heather: For people who need to be around other people and who never want to be alone. They are seeking companionship to share their affairs.

Key Words: Talkative, demanding attention, dislike being alone, lonely.

Human Indications: Helps when preoccupied with their ailments and problems.

Holly: For those who are sometimes attacked by thoughts of jealousy, envy, revenge, or suspicion. Within themselves, they suffer much, when there is no justification for feeling so unhappy.

Key Words: Envy, jealousy, hate, insecurity, suspicious, aggressive, needy, and in need of compassion.

Human Indication: When a person needs to overcome the feelings of envy, jealousy, hate, and suspicion.

Honeysuckle: For those who live too much in the past, perhaps when times were much happier. To help those memories of lost friends or ambitions which are no longer present.

Key Words: Homesickness, nostalgia, and bereavement.

Human Indications: For overattachment of memories (good or bad), cannot let go of the past, and homesick.

Hornbeam: For those who doubt they possess either the physical or mental strength to carry the burden of life placed upon them. Everyday affairs seem too much to accomplish, though they generally succeed in fulfilling their tasks. Those who feel some part of their minds or bodies need to be strengthened before they can easily fulfill their work.

Key Words: Weary, bored, tired, needs strength, overworked, procrastination, and doubting their abilities.

Human Indication: For weariness, more mental than physical. "Monday morning" feeling with a sense of staleness and lack of variety in life.

Impatiens: For those who are quick in thought and action and wish for all things to be done without any hesitation or delay. They find it difficult to be patient around people who are slow, as they consider it wrong and a waste of time, trying to make such people quicker in all ways. When ill, they are very anxious for a hasty recovery. They prefer to work and think alone so that they can do everything at their own speed.

Key Words: Impatient, irritated, nervy, frustrated, fidgety, accident-prone, and hasty.

Human Indication: Suitable for people who are easily agitated or irritated. They speak and think quickly; they are energetic but tense.

Larch: For those who do not consider themselves as good or as capable as those around them, who expect failure, who feel they will never be a success; this usually becomes a self-fulfilling prophecy by their never even attempting to succeed.

Key Words: Lack of confidence, feelings of inferiority, depressed, discouraged.

Human Indication: For one who needs more self-confidence.

Mimulus: For those who have a fear of worldly things, illness, pain, accidents, poverty, fear of the dark, of being alone, or of misfortune; the fears of everyday life. These people quietly and secretly bear their dread, not freely sharing these feelings with others.

Key Words: Fear, blushing, stammering, shyness, timid, sensitive, lacking courage.

Human Indication: Fear of known things, fear of being alone, fear of spiders, fear of the dark, fear of flying.

Mustard: Those who are prone to times of gloom and despair, as though a cold dark cloud overshadows them, hiding the light and joy in their life. It may not be possible to give any reasonable explanation for such attacks. Under these conditions, it is almost impossible to feel happy or cheerful.

Key Words: Depression, deep gloom for no reason.

Human Indications: When feeling depressed for no reason, like a dark cloud that destroys normal cheerfulness.

Oak: For those who are struggling and fighting strongly to get well or in connection with the affairs of their daily lives. They will go on trying one thing after another, though their case may seem hopeless. They will fight on. They are disconnected from themselves if illness interferes with their duties or helping others. They are brave people fighting against great difficulties without loss of hope or effort.

Key Words: Exhaustion, overworked, workaholic, fatigued, over-achiever.

Human Indication: When one is exhausted but keeps on struggling.

Olive: Those who have suffered much mentally and physically and feel so exhausted and weary that they have no strength to make any additional effort. Activities of daily living are very difficult for them without any pleasure.

Key Words: Lack of energy, fatigue, and convalescence.

Human Indication: When a person is exhausted with no reserve strength or energy.

Pine: For those who blame themselves. Even when successful, they feel they could have done better and are never satisfied with their decisions.

Key Words: Guilt, self-reproach, humble, apologetic, shame, unworthy, and undeserving.

Human Indication: When a person feels guilty even though there is no basis for any wrongdoing and destroys the possibility of deriving any joy out of living.

Red Chestnut: For those who find it difficult not to be anxious for other people. Often, they have ceased to worry about themselves.

Key Words: Worried, over-concerned, fear

Human Indication: When a person feels over-concerned and worried for others.

Rock Rose: The remedy for an emergency even when there appears to be no hope. In a serious accident, sudden illness, when the person is very frightened or terrified, or if the condition is serious enough to cause great fear to those around them. If the person is not conscious, one can moisten their lips with this remedy.

Key Words: Frozen, fear, and terror.

Human Indication: When a person feels terror or frightened, like after a nightmare. The feeling that one cannot react or move.

Rock Water: Those who are very strict in their way of living, denying themselves of the many pleasures in life because they fear that they might interfere with their work. They are very hard on themselves. They wish to be well, strong, and active. Willing to do anything that will keep them that way. They hope to serve as examples by appealing to others, who may then follow their ideas and be better as a result.

Key Words: Self-repression, self-denial, self-perfection, overworked, self-sacrificing, and opinionated.

Human Indications: Too strict and sets too high of a standard for themselves, to the point of self-domination and self-martyrdom.

Scleranthus: Those who suffer much from being unable to decide between two things; first one thing seems to be the right decision, then the other. They are usually quiet people who bear their difficulties alone, as they are not inclined to discuss them with others.

Key Words: Indecision, imbalance, uncertainty, and dizziness.

Human Indication: When a person suffers from indecision when faced with two choices.

Star of Bethlehem: For a person in great distress, which, for a time, produces great unhappiness such as the shock of bad news, the loss of someone dear, the fright following an accident, etc. This remedy can bring comfort to those who can be difficult to console.

Key Words: Trauma, aftereffects of shock, and post-traumatic stress.

Human Indication: For aftereffects of trauma or traumatic experience.

Sweet Chestnut: For those moments which happen to some people when the anguish is so great it seems unbearable. When the mind or body feels it can no longer tolerate the utmost limit of its endurance, and that now it must give way. When it seems, there is nothing but destruction and annihilation left to face.

Key Words: Extreme mental anguish, hopelessness, despair, and intense sorrow.

Human Indication: When a person feels hopeless, despair, or intense sorrow and feels destroyed.

Vervain: Those with fixed principles and ideas that they are confidant are right and rarely change. They have a great wish to convert those around them to their views of life. They are strong-willed and have much courage when they are convinced of those things that they wish to teach. In illness, they struggle on after many would have given up the fight to get better.

Key Words: Over-enthusiasm, hyperactive, fanatical, and high-strung

Human Indication: For people who are strong-willed and high-strung with minds that race ahead of events.

Vine: For very capable people, certain of their ability, confident of success. Being so assured that they think it would be for the benefit of others if they could be persuaded to do things as they do or as they are certain is right. Even in illness, they direct their attendants. They may be of great value in an emergency.

Key Words: Domineering, inflexible, very capable, gifted, bullying, and aggressive.

Human Indication: For those who dominate others. They know better than anyone else and will put others down.

Walnut: For those who have definite ideals and ambitions in life and are fulfilling them, but on rare occasions are tempted to be led away from their ideas, aims, and works by the enthusiasm, convictions, or strong opinions of others. This remedy gives constancy and protection from outside influences.

Key Words: Change, link breaker, menopause, puberty, moving, let go of the past, and protection.

Human Indication: Protection from outside influences and energies. Helps one adjust to major changes.

Water Violet: For those in health and illness who like to be alone. Very quiet people who move about without noise; are aloof, leave people alone, and go their own way. Often clever and talented. Their calmness is often a blessing to those around them.

Key Words: Proud, aloof, lonely, anti-social, disdainful, condescending, private, and self-reliant.

Human Indication: People who feel lonely because they tend to be proud and anti-social.

White Chestnut: For those who cannot prevent thoughts, ideas, or arguments which they do not desire from entering their minds, usually at such times when the interest of the moment is not strong enough to keep the mind full. Thoughts that worry and still remain or will return if for a time are thrown out. They seem to circle 'round and 'round and cause mental torture. The presence of such unpleasant thoughts drives out peace and interferes with being able to focus on the work or pleasures of the day.

Key Words: Repeated unwanted thoughts, mental arguments, concentration, sleeplessness, and insomnia.

Human Indication: When a person's mind is cluttered with thoughts or mindful arguments, which make it difficult to sleep.

Wild Oat: Those who have ambitions to do something of prominence in life, who wish to have much experience, and to enjoy all that is possible for them, taking life to the fullest. Their difficulty is in determining what occupation to follow, as their ambitions are strong, but they have no calling which appeals to them above all others. This may cause delay and dissatisfaction.

Key Words: Crossroads in life, decision-making, lack of clarity, drifting in life.

Human Indication: When a person is uncertain of a correct path in life. This remedy is helpful when one needs to make important decisions.

Wild Rose: Those without apparently sufficient reason become resigned to all that happens and just glide through life, take it as it is, without any effort to improve things and find some joy. They have surrendered to the struggle of life without complaint.

Key Words: Apathy, resignation, lost motivation, and lack of ambition.

Human Indication: For anyone who is resigned to an unpleasant situation, whether it be illness, work, or a monotonous life.

Willow: For those who have suffered adversity or misfortune and find it difficult to accept, without complaint or resentment, since they judge life mainly by the success it brings. They feel they have not deserved so great a trial—that it was unjust—and they become embittered. They often take less interest and are less active in things they previously enjoyed.

Key Words: Feel self-pity, resentment, short-changed, a “poor me” attitude, irritable, believe life is not fair to them, sulking, grumbling, bitter, complaining, and casting blame.

Human Indication: When a person feels resentment, self-pity, and bitterness. This remedy applies to a person who would like to regain a sense of humor and proportion.

Please note that these remedies do not contain pharmacologically relevant remnants of the original flower and are considered safe to use in combination with other medications, as well as by pregnant women, children, babies, and the elderly. However, it has been suggested that these remedies could be dangerous to recovering alcoholics due to their alcohol content. Also, with the exception of Rescue Remedy (below), the use of manufactured combination remedies is frowned upon by The Bach Centre, which is considered the leading authority on the use of these remedies, rationalizing that due to each person's metabolic individuality, it is not practical to make a "one-size fits all" combination remedy for individuals. However, as previously mentioned, the one exception is the Rescue Remedy.

The Rescue Remedy: This is Dr. Bach's most famous flower essence formula. This remedy is one of the world's best-known natural stress relief formulas. Effective in virtually any situation that causes stress or anxiety, it helps restore a sense of calm and control. During my many years in practice, I kept this remedy in my office, and it came in handy, especially for patients suffering from anxiety. I also kept it with me when attending funeral services. Invariably, a few drops on the tongue would help a person in mourning cope with their loss of a loved one. The most dramatic result I noticed was when I gave it to my daughter, who was 17 at the time. She was in a very serious car accident, and when I arrived at the Emergency Room, she was hysterical, with a large laceration on the top of her skull, which she would not allow the doctor to suture. I put a few drops of Rescue Remedy on her tongue, and she calmed down immediately, allowing the doctor to suture her up. This remedy is composed of Cherry Plum, Clematis, Impatiens, Rock Rose, and Star of Bethlehem.

The fact that I purposely elaborated in great detail the benefits and indications of all 38 of the Bach Flower remedies and the Rescue Remedy hopefully conveys to the reader the importance of these remedies, especially when all other modalities have failed to elicit favorable results. These remedies were among the most valuable modalities I employed while in practice, especially with patients trying to take responsibility for their health. Even though they were practicing a healthy lifestyle, they were still saddled with their condition. Invariably, the missing piece which was not being addressed was the emotional component of their health phenomenon. Supplementing these difficult cases with the Bach Flower remedies, in addition to having them read the affirmation, "The Script" from the book, *Feelings Buried Alive Never Die*, went a long way in helping them cope, if not relieving them of their condition.

Chapter Seventeen

Homeopathy

Homeopathy: This is a system of alternative medicine created in 1796 by Samuel Hahnemann. Based on his doctrine, "like cures like," ("homolos" in Greek means "similar"; "pathos" means "suffering") a claim that states that a substance which causes symptoms of disease in healthy people would cure similar symptoms in sick people. For example, red onions make your eyes water, which is why it is used as a remedy for allergies. This system of healing had an interesting history. Dr. Hahnemann graduated from medical school in 1779 and started his practice of medicine. He soon began his homeopathic experiments in 1790 due to his disillusionment with such common medical practices, which included purging, bloodletting, and toxic chemicals. At one point, he gave up his own medical practice to begin working as a chemist while translating medical texts. When Dr. Hahnemann began working on a project to translate Materia Medica, by William Cullen, into German, he began his quest for a better way of providing healthcare using the principle of "Similars." While working on this project, he became fascinated with a species of South American tree bark (cinchona), which was being used to treat malaria-induced fever. He ingested the bark and discovered it caused symptoms similar to malaria. He continued his research into "cures" and the idea of "similar suffering." He began to compile his findings. "*simila similibus curentur,*" the Latin phrase for "let like be cured by like," the primary principle of homeopathy.

Students of Dr. Hahnemann founded the first homeopathic medical school in the United States in the late 1800s. It gained great recognition because of its success in treating many disease epidemics rampant at the time, including scarlet fever, typhoid, cholera, and yellow fever. The school's method of treatment became very popular in the early 1900s. At that time, there were 22 homeopathic medical schools, 100 homeopathic hospitals, and over 1,000 homeopathic pharmacies. Boston University, Stanford University, and New York Medical College were among those educational institutions that were teaching homeopathy. However, it was not long after this (the early 1920s) that many schools closed. The schools closed mostly due to a decline of homeopathy's popularity, greatly affected by the American Medical Association. This was around the time when drug companies began releasing drugs that were easy to administer to patients, a trend that also contributed to the decline of homeopathy.

Although the United States experienced a dwindling of homeopathy in the 20th century, other nations, including countries in Europe and Asia, were experiencing a steady growth of homeopathic teachings and interest. Today nearly all French pharmacies sell homeopathic remedies and medicines. Homeopathy also has a solid following in Russia, India, Switzerland, Mexico, Germany, Netherlands, Italy, England, and South Africa.

Homeopathy is also rising again in the United States. This resurgence has been documented by the National Center of Homeopathy in Virginia. Doctors, scientists, researchers (over 300 research papers published in esteemed journals such as *Lancet*), corporations, and the general public are all responsible for the accelerated expansion in the interest of homeopathic products, research, and educational initiatives.

A homeopathic Doctor must undertake many years of study and clinical experience. Homeopaths can be medical doctors, and in the United States, many homeopaths are chiropractors, naturopaths, osteopaths, nurse practitioners, dentists, and veterinarians. Many training programs exist in North America today. In Alexandria, Virginia, the National Center for Homeopathy can provide an updated list of new and developing programs in the United States.

I felt it incumbent upon myself to give the reader a little history on the philosophy, science, and art of homeopathy because, unfortunately, the average layman either knows very little about homeopathy or considers it quackery because it is not as mainstream as Allopathic Medicine, which is the main healing art in America. I worked very closely with a constitutional homeopathic doctor, Dr. Anthony Aurigemma, for many years while in practice. I would refer patients who were not achieving satisfactory results from our care. Invariably, patients experienced total remission of their conditions when they took the remedies he prescribed for their individual needs.

There are three distinct levels of Homeopathy:

Level One: First Aid

Homeopathy can be used in first aid to safely treat common ailments and occurrences, such as sprains, bruises, minor burns, skin irritations and reactions (including poison ivy, diaper rash, and insect bites), the pain of teething, etc.

Level Two: Acute Homeopathy

Acute health problems are those in which the symptoms will eventually resolve themselves. They are temporary conditions, such as colds, flu, coughs, sprains, etc. A homeopathic remedy can be useful and attractive because it is safe, gentle, and has no harmful side effects. Homeopathy can also be used to assist sensitive conditions such as pregnancy.

Level Three: Constitutional Homeopathy

Constitutional Homeopathy refers to the treatment of a person as a whole, including past and present symptoms, in an attempt to address the underlying cause of the condition.

This is the main difference between Homeopathy, which addresses the cause of a condition, compared to traditional Allopathic medicine, which treats the symptoms. They both play an important role in the healing arts; however, homeopathy is definitely more indicated for chronic conditions due to its holistic approach of treating the whole person. Allopathic medicine excels in emergency care and, when indicated, can administer drugs for patients with end-stage illness to make their remaining days on Earth more comfortable. When accurately implemented, homeopathic constitutional care can elicit a profound healing response. Homeopathy can be extremely effective in treating chronic and long-term health problems. Recurrent ear infections, for example, can be treated with a homeopathic remedy for a longer time to strengthen the body's immune system and prevent future occurrences.

For the reader to better understand homeopathy, let me elaborate on the relationship between symptoms and homeopathy. As stated at the beginning of this work, symptoms are the advanced stage of a condition, not the first stage most people believe. Symptoms are the body's way of signaling that it is out of balance. Without symptoms, a person could have a life-threatening event without any way of identifying it. Many patients had life-threatening diseases such as cancer who have reported that they had not suffered from a cold or flu in years prior to their diagnosis. The explanation was probably not that they didn't have infections during this period, but more likely that their bodies were unable to fight these infections by producing necessary symptom indications. Many conventional drugs try to inhibit and suppress symptoms, sometimes leading to even more serious problems.

Conventional (Allopathic) physicians do not usually recognize the new series of symptoms related to the old. Thus, they treat them as new and unrelated problems.

A classic example would be a person suffering from candidiasis (yeast overgrowth in the gut). In the early stage of this condition, most patients would consult with their physician complaining of digestive issues such as bloating, possible heartburn, upper and lower bowel gas. Depending on the severity of the symptoms, the physician might recommend some over-the-counter treatments which would not require a prescription or possibly something stronger if indicated. While the prescribed treatment may alleviate the symptoms (though in many cases the symptoms persist), the underlying cause of the condition is not addressed (usually a lifestyle issue such as a diet high in refined carbs (from sugar products such as baked goods, soda, etc.) eventually leading to a more chronic condition due to untreated yeast overgrowth.

The patient will start complaining of additional symptoms depending on which system of the body has been affected by the yeast overgrowth. This condition can cause perforations in the gut wall (known as intestinal permeability), which becomes an avenue for the candida (yeast) to enter the bloodstream and infiltrate different systems of the body (e.g., the respiratory, genito-urinary, and nervous system, including the brain, with each affected system producing its own set of symptoms).

When the affected patient consults their physician with a new set of symptoms, it is treated as a new condition altogether, allowing the original unaddressed condition to become even more chronic and very debilitating.

Did you know that a fever is the body's attempt to activate the immune system's white blood cells and defend itself against infections? If a person is given a fever-suppressing medication too soon to fight the fever, they will be less able to fight the disease. These drugs are given if the fever is too high due to a very virulent pathogen, which can cause a convulsive state and being quite serious if a very high fever is not treated accordingly. Homeopathy does not seek to suppress symptoms. Homeopathy's goal is to recognize and remove the underlying cause of these symptoms. This is why a homeopathic doctor will work toward understanding the whole person, including their body, mind, and emotional state, before prescribing a remedy.

The actual remedies are very small doses. For the most part, the amounts are derived from extremely small quantities of nanoparticles of substances derived from plants, animals, minerals, and even bacteria. They are prepared using a specific process, including dilution of potentization and vigorous shaking (called succussion).

The more the dose is diluted, the more powerful the medicine (i.e., a 30 C potency means it is cut 30 times and is thirty times stronger than a 1C potency. Also, a dose can be as high as 10M, which is diluted 10,000 times. A single dose at this high potency can last for weeks or months and even years occasionally.) The good news here is that the constitutional level is the only level that requires a homeopathic doctor.

Both the first aid and acute levels of care can be treated with first aid homeopathic kits. We kept one in our home, and believe me; it came in very handy with five children. A kit will usually contain 50 remedies and can be upgraded to as many as 100 remedies chosen for acute and emergency situations. A kit will usually include a list of some common uses of each remedy. If interested, which I suggest, you can go online to purchase a kit from Boiron USA. www.Boiron.com.

Here is a list of some of the more essential remedies and their usage found in a kit:

Aconite: Best used when a cold or cough comes on suddenly, especially after getting a chill. A good remedy for fear or fright, like after a nightmare, especially when sleeping away from home for the first time. One to two doses a few hours apart should do the trick.

Arnica: The pre-eminent remedy for injuries, falls, bruises, concussions, strains, and sprains. No remedy kit should be without this one. Depending on the severity of the injury, one pellet three times a day for a day or two should be enough to get you or other members of the family good to go. It is also available in a cream for topical application. Remember me sharing the story about my daughter and her car accident? Besides being hysterical, she had a large, elevated, egg size bruise on her forehead that disappeared overnight while she was in the hospital with a topical application of Arnica to the area.

Apis: The first remedy to think of with stings or bites, whether a wasp, bee, mosquito or red ant. If the area is red, hot, or itchy and feels better with cold, Apis is the one for you. Apis can also be used as a preventative when going camping or hiking if prone to bites.

Arsenicum Album: Especially for those going away from home, an upset stomach can ruin the day. Whether it be from food poisoning, anxiety, or a mild bug, Arsenicum is usually the most likely remedy to help.

Belladonna: This is a good remedy for the first sign of fever with red hot skin. It can also be used with a sunburn; take every hour for three hours to really get the heat out and the skin healing.

Calendula cream: A must for any First Aid kit! It is applied topically to scrapes. Make sure they are well-cleaned before applying. It is an excellent and effective natural alternative to over-the-counter creams at the drug store.

Gelsemium: The first remedy to think of for summer colds, especially if the symptoms are vague, where the person is chilly, has little thirst, and low energy. Try one dose every 12 hours for three doses.

Hypericum perforatum: Used for nerve pain such as sciatica, back pain, a stubbed toe, a finger slammed in a door, a fall on the tailbone with characteristic nerve pain: shooting, sharp, and tingling. One to six doses, depending on the severity of pain, in 24 hours should do the trick. It can also be applied topically to injured areas, as well as taken internally.

Ignatia: It is great for kids who leave home on camping trips only to get homesick. Should stop the crying and sighing and missing home in a flash. One dose should do the job.

Ledum: This is a good remedy to think of with a puncture wound, such as stepping on a nail or something sharp. Also helpful for bites if Apis does not work or is not indicated, as Ledum bites feel cold to the touch. It is also good for large bruises if Arnica does not help. The best remedy for a black eye if used immediately after contact to the eye socket.

Rhus tox: This remedy has two very useful indications. The first is with a poison ivy rash. The second is particularly useful for sprains or strains, especially when the joint is stiff in the morning and feels better upon movement. Use Rhus tox following Arnica when Arnica no longer provides any benefit. Take one pellet every two hours for three doses.

Ruta: Easily confused with Rhus-tox for use in sprains. It seems to have more of an affinity for tendons. If unsure, try Rhus tox first, and if no improvement is noticed, begin a remedy of Ruta.

Silicea: Also known as Silica. This remedy can sometimes be used to encourage splinters to be expelled. Give it a try!

I would be remiss if I failed to mention the benefits of my favorite acute homeopathic remedy. It is called Oscillococcinum. This remedy offers dramatic relief from the onset of Influenza (the flu) if taken in the early stages of the condition. I recommended this remedy to patients, family, and friends for many years with very gratifying outcomes. At the very least, if taken at the early onset of symptoms (body aches, headache, fever, chills, and fatigue), the duration and severity of this condition would be markedly reduced. It can be purchased at most, if not all, of the major pharmaceutical outlets. It would be wise for the reader to buy this remedy prior to the flu season since administering it as soon as symptoms manifest themselves will produce the optimum benefit as far as the abatement of the symptoms is concerned.

Homeopathic Cell Salts

Cell salts stimulate the body's natural healing mechanisms to satisfy any mineral deficiencies and imbalances in the body. Dr. Wilhelm Schuessler, a German doctor who discovered these cell salts, established the theory of Biochemic medicine in 1873, which states that deficiencies in these minerals are the source of common health problems. Through his research, he determined that cell salts derived from these minerals give the body what it needs to treat illness and to be well. Cell Salts are made from the minerals required by our cells and bring balance and health to muscle tissue and restore overall cell function. Combining the principles of biochemistry and homeopathy, he formulated these cell salts in homeopathic micro-doses, making them safe for the whole family, including children two years of age and older. They are safe to use with other medications and are available in quick-dissolving tablets.

Here are the 12 Cell Salts and their usage:

1. Calc. Fluor: Colds, hemorrhoids, and chapped skin

2. Calc. Phos: Fatigue and sore throats

3. Calc. Sulph: Colds, sore throats, and acne

4. Ferrum. Phos: Fevers, minor swelling, and colds.

5. Kali. Mur: Colds, sore throats, and runny noses

6. Kali. Phos: Stress, simple nervous tension, and headaches

7. Kali. Sulph: Colds and skin eruptions

8. Mag. Phos: Muscle cramps and pains

9. Nat. Mur: Headaches, colds, heartburn, gastric upset, or distress.

10. Nat. Phos: Indigestion, gas, and hyperacidity

11. Nat. Sulph: Flu, nausea, and vomiting

12. Silica: Skin eruptions, brittle hair, and nails

Combination Remedies:

Bioplasma: A combination of all 12 cell salts to balance and support cellular health and function.

Biochemic Phosphates: Contain five cell salts (calcium, Ferrum, kali, magnesium, and naturam), phosphates which optimize nervous system balance and function. It is used to treat nervous exhaustion, irritability, and sleeplessness.

Chapter Eighteen

Additional Health Suggestions

Hydrotherapy:

Water therapy has been used through the ages as a healing modality by many cultures. Countries such as New Zealand, Iceland, and Italy are known for their naturally occurring hot springs where people can take advantage of the mineral-rich waters. Similarly, the use of cold water can also positively affect one's health, called cryotherapy. Many athletes will submerge themselves in ice-cold water to alleviate muscle strains induced by exercise or physical exertion. The benefits of submerging the body in water, regardless of the temperature, have been proven scientifically to upregulate the mind, spirit, and body.

Bathing has many proven scientific effects. Bathing is good for your heart! We are talking about a warm bath that will cause your heart to beat faster, dilate your blood vessels, slightly lower blood pressure, and increase your circulation throughout the body, giving it a little healthy workout. CAREFUL! Bathing in water that is too hot can put unnecessary strain on the heart, especially if there is already a pre-existing heart condition.

Bathing can upregulate lung capacity. Submerging the body in water up to the chest can positively impact oxygen intake due to the warm temperature of the water and the pressure it places on the chest and lungs. The heart beating a little faster from the warm water will also improve oxygen intake. Sinuses may also clear from the steam being emitted from the warm water.

Bathing affects the brain and nervous system. Submerging in warm water can reduce pain and inflammation, have a calming effect on the nervous system, reduce stress and anxiety, and improve mood. We now know how harmful stress is to the body and the mind and spirit. Hydrotherapy has been proven to help people suffering from Multiple Sclerosis. Again, water temperature should be more on the tepid side because a high water temperature can impair the ability of demyelinated nerves (loss of nerve coverings) to conduct electrical impulses. Additionally, warm water can gently relieve the spine of pain and discomfort. Hydrotherapy also provides postural stability and can help alleviate symptoms associated with such conditions as Parkinson's Disease.

Bathing can benefit muscles, joints, and bones. Exercising in water will have a low impact on the joints, muscles, and bones while providing some resistance to afford an adequate workout. This type of water exercise called aqua aerobics is ideal for the elderly. Aquatic exercise can also alleviate some of the discomfort associated with osteoarthritis without any adverse effects or aggravation of symptoms.

Bathing can improve Gastrointestinal health. Although baths are not advised directly after eating, taking warm baths can help digestion by increasing blood circulation. The heat of a warm bath can also alleviate pain associated with hemorrhoids or anal fissures by relaxing the anal sphincter.

Bathing can enhance the birthing process. It is well documented that women in the first stages of labor can maximize relaxation and minimize pain when immersed in warm water, allowing them to focus on birthing their babies and progressing their labor. There are no adverse effects to either the mother or child during labor or after the child's birth.

These are some of the main benefits of bathing (hydrotherapy). To enhance the benefit of bathing in a warm tub of water, one can add some Epsom salt which is high in Magnesium. Epson salt is great for muscle relaxation, especially in the lower back region. For an additional benefit, add different oil essences to the bath. My favorite is adding a few drops of Lavender oil to my bath, which is very relaxing due to its ability to lower the stress hormone cortisol.

Women prone to bladder infections should address this issue with a doctor specializing in integrative medicine to correct the problem before using hydrotherapy.

Negative Ionizers:

Whenever someone hears a word preceded by the adjective "negative" concerning the human body, it usually conjures up an image of something deleterious or harmful to this magnificent creation. However, where negative ionizers are concerned, quite the opposite is true. For those of you who have no idea what I am talking about, allow me to explain.

Did you ever wonder why the air is so fresh when you go up into the mountains or sit on the beach, especially close to where the waves crash onto the surf, or after a storm, or standing near a waterfall? Well, my friend, wonder no more. You see, the wind blowing through the leaves of trees high up in the mountains, as well as the waves crashing down on the surf, or the aftereffects of a storm, or just being close to a waterfall, have one thing in common. They create negative ions, electrically charged atoms (meaning they have an extra electron attached). One of the main benefits of negative ions is that they clear the air of airborne allergens such as mold spores, bacteria, viruses, pollen, dust mites, pet dander, and smoke, literally causing these allergens to become too heavy to remain airborne, thus, preventing someone from breathing them in. They accomplish this feat by attaching themselves to positively charged particles that have lost one or more electrons. These positive ions are harmful to the body.

Fortunately, they are neutralized through this attachment by giving the positively charged particle an extra electron, causing the positive ion to become heavier. The negative ions form a protective circle around the body to prevent these allergens from entering the body via the air passages and invading the body. The lack of these negative ions can cause headaches, possible nausea and precipitate one's allergies. This event is usually more demonstrable in overcrowded areas, confined spaces such as offices, industrial areas, schools, and cars, which can have a high concentration of these unhealthy positive ions. Negative ions are also present in our bodies. It has been scientifically proven that these negative ions contribute to one's well-being and overall health.

Some of their benefits include:

1. They neutralize free radicals, which can be very harmful to the body as you probably know.

2. They revitalize cell metabolism.

3. They enhance immune function.

4. They purify the blood.

5. They balance the autonomic nervous system, promoting deep sleep and healthy digestion

(Source: kiflow.com).

Now, you might be thinking, is there any other way you can still receive the benefits of negative ions since you are not fortunate enough to be in a natural environment such as the ocean or the mountains except when on vacations? Well, there is good news. You can purchase a negative ion air purifier, which will help you breathe cleaner, healthier air (great for asthmatics) and protect yourself from exposure to allergens, as was previously described. There are many different types of purifiers on the market. I have a system that keeps my entire living space imbued with "fresh air."

You can even buy a pendant to wear around your neck to keep the air around you clean as it emits negative ions constantly to neutralize the positive ions in the space around you. Just take advantage of the World Wide Web and check it out if it sounds like a modality you might want to have.

Note: Please be advised that some pendants may expose an individual to radiation exposure since some pendants contain trace amounts of radioactive material according to the IEMA (Illinois Emergency Management Agency (anyone interested can go to https://www2.illinois.gov/iema/info/Pages/05158.aspx).

A pendant that I would suggest was designed by Dr. Valerie Nelson, MD, MBA, which is comprised of 30 + homeopathic frequencies to neutralize EMF (electro-magnetic frequencies) radiation which we are constantly exposed to in our daily environment (emf's are produced by anything that has voltage such as lamps, electrical wiring, electrical outlets, electric appliances, and electric cords).

Far Infra-Red Sauna:

I mentioned earlier that I would be suggesting different at-home health options that may prove useful in improving one's quality and quantity of life while avoiding an undue financial expense. If it is within your budget, I would highly recommend this particular home therapy, which I found so beneficial personally that I eventually installed another unit at our health center. Currently, many different companies are manufacturing Far Infra-Red Saunas, and a single-person unit can be purchased for under $2,000.

Here are some of the known benefits of this type of home therapy.

1. Unlike a traditional sauna that heats the surrounding air at very high temperatures, 80% of the heat emitted by far infra-red sauna heats the body directly at a much lower temperature.

2. The warming effect on the body stimulates the cardiovascular, immune, and lymphatic systems.

3. The body is heated more directly instead of the air; one sweats more profusely, upregulating detoxification.

4. Studies show sweat analyzed from this type of sauna contains 4-5 times higher toxin content than sweat from a regular sauna, which demonstrates improved detoxification.

5. It enhances weight loss by the ability of their wavelengths to penetrate fat cells, which causes them to vibrate, thus increasing metabolism.

6. Joint and muscle pain relief.

7. Stress reduction.

8. Reduces inflammation.

9. Increases mitochondria function, producing more ATP (energy).

10. Improves sleep.

For the most part, far infrared saunas are considered safe; however, patients should check with their doctors to make sure there are no contraindications in their particular case, such as a genetic predisposition to overheating, which is rare. Users should also hydrate before and after a sauna session to replace electrolytes lost from sweating.

Superfoods:

I consider these foods a *must* for one's diet, including fruits, vegetables, nuts, seeds, and spices. However, I would first like to discuss a process that has been used for ages to naturally preserve food that is also beneficial to one's health. The process is known as Fermentation. Many cultures realize the health benefits of consuming fermented foods. Different cultures are known for their different fermented specialties. The following is a brief description of some of the more popular fermented foods and their country of origin.

Sauerkraut: (Means "sour cabbage" in German). However, it

originated in China.

Kefir: This is a fermented milk drink that has been in existence for thousands of years that originated in the Caucasus mountains in the former Soviet Union, where the drink is fermented in bags of animal hides.

Kombucha: This is a ferment that originated in China and has been around for over 2,000 years. It was developed during the Tsin Dynasty and was known as the "Tea of Immortality."

Kimchi: This is a fermented staple in the Korean diet, derived from salted vegetables such as cabbage and Korean radish, which can be made with a variety of seasonings, including scallions, ginger, and garlic, to name just a few ingredients.

Yogurt: This is a very popular type of ferment which originated in Turkey in the seventh century A.D.

Apple Cider Vinegar: One of my favorite ferments originated in Rome and Greece at about the same time. It has numerous beneficial effects on the body, including weight loss and providing remedies for ailments such as heartburn, leg cramps, chronic fatigue, sore throat, high cholesterol, constipation, inflammation, bad breath, hiccups, fibromyalgia, and sinus congestion, to name a few attributes of this wonderful elixir. You can get the book, *The Apple Cider Vinegar Miracle - 81 Ways to Naturally Cleanse Your Body and House and More* by The Alternative Daily.

Why do so many different cultures had some type of fermented food as a staple in their diets? What was the "magic elixir" ingredient they all had in common, which was beneficial to their health? The common denominator was the presence of probiotics which are produced in fermentation. Probiotics are (live) good bacteria that are essential to one's health. But equally important are the lesser-known prebiotics that is also a by-product of the fermentation process. Prebiotics are the non-digestible fiber that acts as a fertilizer, if you will, to upregulate the growth of the good bacteria in the body. The microbiome of good bacteria in the gut needs food to survive and achieve all their many functions, and the perfect way to feed them is with prebiotics. When you hear the term “bacteria,” you may first think of the negative "bad guys" that are harmful to your health. However, we are refering to the good bacteria, which aid the body with digestion and the production of nutrients such as the B vitamins, namely biotin, B12, choline, and thiamine.

Good bacteria also aid the production of neurotransmitters. Neurotransmitters such as serotonin and GABA are the “feel good" neurotransmitters used by the brain to help relieve symptoms of insomnia, anxiety, and depression. They also act as enzymes to break down food for better assimilation of nutrients in the gut. They help maintain a good balance between the good and bad bacteria in the gut microbiome.

Hundreds of scientific papers have been published touting the benefits of probiotics. Additional benefits include upregulating the immune system and alleviating diarrhea, which can be very debilitating if not corrected. As a side note, research has shown that different strains of good bacteria have different health benefits. It behooves one to purchase probiotics with many different strains to receive the maximum benefit from them. Usually, the live strains of good bacteria that are refrigerated are more beneficial. Ideally, you should consume at least 10 Billion CFUs (Colony Forming Units) daily.

So, now that we know some of the benefits of fermented foods, the process should be explained to afford you a better understanding and appreciation of this process. The technical definition of fermentation is how carbohydrates are chemically broken down by enzymes, yeast, bacteria, or other microorganisms. For the most part, the process typically involves effervescence and heat in the absence of oxygen, known as an anaerobic phenomenon. As a side note, the word ferment is Latin meaning, "to leaven or to rise,” which usually happens when yeast, for example, is introduced into the dough.

Note: Fermented foods are contra-indicated for people suffering from a condition known as Candidiasis, a situation where there is an over-proliferation of yeast in the gut. Unfortunately, these fermented foods can also trigger the reproduction of more yeast, which in turn will exacerbate Candidiasis

Some of the causes are diets high in sugar or antibiotics, or birth control pills. If gone untreated, the side effects can be devastating to one's health, potentially attacking all the systems of the body once it penetrates the gut lining and gets into the circulatory system. In my practice, I treated many patients for this condition. It usually goes undetected because the symptoms can mimic other conditions. If you have health issues that have not been properly addressed by well-meaning professionals, despite you doing your due diligence, you might want to consider reading up on this condition.

The Yeast Connection, by Dr. Thomas Crook, contains a subjective questionnaire that results in a score that suggests a slight or strong possibility of having this condition. Understand, as previously mentioned, the fermentation process also produces prebiotics, which, in essence, are food for the probiotics as well as any yeast or bad bacteria that might be present. So let me repeat, if there is already an overgrowth of yeast present in the gut, adding fermented food to the diet can only make Candidiasis worse.

I used a simple test in my office for many years to determine if a patient had Candidiasis. About five years ago, this simple test was made popular on the Dr. Oz show. It is called the "Spit Test" and is now even available to watch on YouTube. Visit https://www.youtube.com/watch?v=6WIpCvBwszg

During the testing period, avoid any dairy products for ten days, then spit into a glass of water at room temperature first thing in the morning. Allow the saliva to stand for 45 minutes. Then, check for either "stringy, leg-like" projections radiating down from the spittle, cloudy saliva at the bottom of the glass, or opaque specks of saliva in the middle of the glass. Any of these three manifestations are a good indication that there may be a Candida overgrowth present and warrants further investigation by a holistic professional who has experience treating this disorder. I realize I went off on a bit of a tangent, but I would have been remiss if I did not elaborate on the fermentation subject. Now, let's continue with the subject of superfoods.

Note: The following information presented by Dianne Onstad (*Whole Food Companion*).

***Almonds:** (a demulcent, emollient, see below) They have special healing and protective qualities. They are the most alkaline of all nuts, although still slightly acidic. Almonds are particularly valuable as an essential building food for those who are underweight. Their high fat, carbohydrate, and protein content make them an ideal food for strengthening the body when there is no need to worry about increasing the supply of fat. Almonds contain a small amount of Amygdalin, better known as laetrile, which has anti-carcinogenic properties.

N.B. A demulcent or emollient is an agent that is soothing to the intestinal tract, usually of an oily nature, and which provides a protective coating and allays irritation. It soothes and softens the part to which it is applied, acting to relieve irritation.

***Apple:** Apples are naturally anti-toxic. They can modify the intestinal tract by reactivating the beneficial bacteria that generally flourish there. Apples are a highly digestible alkaline food. They contain both malic acid and tartaric acid, which help remove impurities in the liver and inhibit the growth of ferments and disease-producing bacteria in the digestive tract. The pectin in apples helps make it an excellent intestinal "broom," working as a bulking agent, gently pushing through the digestive tract and cleansing it along the way. Pectin also combines with radioactive residues, removing them from the body, along with lead, mercury, and other toxic heavy metals.

***Avocado:** One of the world's most perfect foods. It has a perfectly balanced PH, neither acidic or alkaline, and is easy to digest. Rich in mineral elements that regulate body functions and stimulate growth. Noteworthy, avocados are high in iron and copper content, which aid in red blood cell regeneration and the prevention of nutritional anemia—one of the most valuable organic fat and protein sources.

***Bananas:** One of the neatest and most convenient packaged foods and a powerhouse of nutritional energy. Fully ripe bananas are composed of 76% water, 20% sugar, the balance being made up of starch and a large contingent of vitamins and minerals, and a great deal of fiber. Green bananas contain anti-nutrients, proteins that inhibit the actions of amylase, an enzyme involved in the digestion of starches and other complex carbohydrates. Wait until bananas are fully ripe before eating.

Anti-fungal and antibiotic principles are found both in the pulp and peel of fully ripened bananas. Bananas are considered a good prebiotic to feed the good bacteria in the bowel. Their high vitamin and mineral content, especially potassium, benefit the muscular and nervous systems. Their sugars are readily assimilated for use as fuel, and the pectin content helps heal ulcers and lowers blood cholesterol. Bananas are also rich in the amino acid Tryptophan, which is known to promote sleep and contains enzymes that assist in the manufacture of sexual hormones. For those trying to gain weight or build muscle bulk, bananas are a wonderful food (along with appropriate exercise). They are perfect for young children and infants as they are easily digested and can be pureed with water to form a type of milk.

Remember, only use ripened bananas, as unripe bananas can be constipating, while ripened bananas act as laxatives.

***Broccoli:** Raw broccoli contains almost as much calcium as whole milk and is linked to lowering the risk of cancers. Eat raw broccoli so that the chlorophyll will be left to counteract the sulfur compounds that form gas. Broccoli contains abundant pantothenic acid (vitamin B5) and vitamin A, which benefits rough skin. All Brassica genus vegetables contain dithiolethiones, which are a group of compounds with anti-cancer and antioxidant properties. Broccoli also contains indoles, a substance that protects against breast and colon cancer; sulfur, which has antibiotic and anti-viral characteristics; and lutein and zeaxanthin, pigments that protect plants (and thus indirectly humans) from the harmful effects of photo-oxidation by filtering out visible blue light. This family of vegetables also mildly stimulates and detoxifies other tissues of the body.

***Garlic:** Garlic is anti-bacterial, anti-septic, anti-spasmodic, anti-helminthic, carminative, diaphoretic, and expectorant. Garlic is good for heart disease, worms, tumors, headaches, and bites and possessing antibiotic and fungicidal properties. Garlic can lower cholesterol and act as a decongestant. One raw crushed clove contains the antibiotic equivalent of 100,000 units of penicillin and has proven more effective than either penicillin or tetracycline in suppressing certain types of disease-carrying agents. Garlic is most beneficial to the digestive system and has a strong effect on the lymphatic fluid and tissue, aiding in the elimination of noxious wastes. It helps eliminate lead and other heavy metals from the body and rids the alimentary canal (digestive system) of worms and other parasites while boosting immunological functions.

***Lemon juice:** Lemon juice acts as an astringent, antiseptic, stimulates the liver and gall bladder, stirring up any inactive acids and any latent toxic sedimentation that cannot be eliminated in any other way. Lemons contain limonene, are used to dissolve gall stones, and show promise as an anti-cancer agent. Lemons are acidic to taste, but they have a strong alkaline reaction in the body provided that no sugar is added. They destroy putrefactive bacteria in both the intestines and the mouth, and they alleviate flatulence. Potassium content nourishes the brain and nerve cells. Calcium strengthens the body structures and makes healthy teeth. Lemons are also an outstanding source of vitamin C.

***Cabbage:** One of the least expensive vitamin-protective foods and one of the most healthful. Raw cabbage detoxifies the stomach and upper bowels of putrefactive waste, thereby enhancing digestive efficiency and facilitating rapid elimination. It also works to alkalize the body, stimulate the immune system, kill harmful bacteria and viruses, soothe and heal ulcers (contains vitamin U, known to heal ulcers), help prevent cancers and clear up skin complexion. Raw sauerkraut is an excellent cleansing and rejuvenating food for the digestive tract. It promotes nutrient absorption as well as the growth of healthful acidophilus intestinal flora.

Those who feel hot most of the time (i.e., those who like sleeping with a window open, even if in winter), referred to in traditional Chinese medicine as body heat, will do well on cabbage. Its sulfur and iron content will improve circulation which removes heat from the body. It contains Iodine and is an excellent source of vitamin C. The outer leaves contain a high vitamin E concentration and contain at least a third more calcium than the inner leaves. They have anti-cancer, antioxidant properties; indoles, substances that protect the body against breast and colon cancer; and sulfur, which has anti-viral and antibiotic characteristics. This family of vegetables, Brassica, mildly stimulates the liver and other tissues out of stagnancy.

***Cantaloupe melons:** Excellent cleansers and re-hydrators of the body, being over 90% water. They rejuvenate and alkalize the body with their highly mineralized water and aid in elimination. Their Silicon content is high, especially when eaten right down to the rind. Cantaloupes contain the compound adenosine currently being used on heart patients to keep the blood thin and relieve angina attacks. Melons are such perfect foods for humans that they require no digestion whatsoever in the stomach. Instead, they pass quickly through the stomach into the small intestines for digestion and assimilation. This is why it's important always to consume melons alone; do not combine them with other foods that require complex digestion because the melon cannot pass into the small intestine until the digestion of the more complex food is complete. Thus, they sit and stagnate, quickly fermenting and causing gastric distress.

***Cherries:** Cherries are higher than any other food source in natural vitamin C. They are detoxifying, laxative, and are a stimulant. They are a good "spring cleaner" to stimulate and cleanse the digestive system. The darker cherries are more valuable to the system, as they contain a greater quantity of magnesium, iron, and silicon. Cherries are a well-known remedy for gout, arthritis, and rheumatism. Part of their action in rheumatic conditions comes from their ability to eliminate excess body acids. Their high iron content makes them beneficial to the liver, blood, and gallbladder.

***Cayenne Pepper:** An appetizer, digestive stimulant, and tonic. It is one of the strongest stimulants which produces a natural warmth and helps improve circulation. It aids digestion when taken with meals, arouses all the secreting organs, and heals stomach and intestinal ulcers. Cayenne pepper has a cleansing action on the large intestine and sweat glands and helps evacuate the bowels of worms and parasites. Cayenne pepper is good for colds, coughs, and congestion and produces a natural warmth when used as a poultice for pneumonia and other acute congestions. For travelers, a container of red cayenne pepper is sensible protection when traveling in a country where food preparation and serving are not always sanitary. It protects against amoebic dysentery.

***Coconut:** Coconut contains natural iodine necessary to prevent thyroid gland problems. It is warming, sweet, and energizing. Coconut contains calcium, phosphorous, potassium, sodium, zinc, copper, manganese, beta carotene, and vitamins A, B1, B2, B3, B5, B6, B9, C, and E. Coconut is also very rich in MCT (medium-chain triglycerides). MCT is good for nutritional support during training to increase exercise performance, decrease body fat, increase lean muscle mass, and weight loss. MCT can also reduce levels of cholesterol and other fats in the blood called triglycerides.

It is also good cooking oil since it does well at high cooking temperatures.

***Vanilla:** Vanilla is an agent that stimulates the liver to increase bile production, which aids in the digestion of fats in the small intestines (a process known as emulsification), and increases peristalsis, the transit time of digestion for waste elimination.

***Dates:** In early medicine, dates were one of the four fruits renowned for curing throat and chest ailments. Other fruits with similar properties are figs and raisins. Because of their tannin content, dates have been used medicinally as an astringent for intestinal troubles. Dates are heat-producing due to their natural sugar content and give energy to people who engage in physical exercise and hard work. This natural sugar is much better for a person than refined (processed) white sugar. The fiber or cellulose of the date is very soft and will not irritate a sensitive bowel or stomach.

***Dill:** Dill is anti-spasmodic, diuretic, and a stimulant. Dill helps to dispel flatulence, stimulate the appetite, settle indigestion, induce sleep, and increase mother's milk. Chewing dill will clear up halitosis. It makes all food more digestible and has a high vitamin content.

***Cucumber:** Cucumber is an alkaline, non-starchy cooling vegetable rich in minerals that neutralize blood acidosis. Cucumber is a laxative and a diuretic; in fact, it is the best natural diuretic known, and it facilitates excretion of waste through the kidneys, so it does not need to be purged through the skin. Cucumbers help to dissolve uric acid accumulations such as kidney and bladder stones. Among other enzymes, the cucumber contains erepsin, which helps digest proteins; it also helps digestion in general. It destroys worms, especially tapeworms, and its potassium content makes it useful for high and low blood pressure.

***Figs:** Figs are a laxative and restorative. The medical use of figs is almost as ancient as the plant itself, and the fruit has been used to treat nearly every known disease. Figs are restorative and the best food taken by a person weak and debilitated from sickness for a protracted period. In the past, athletes and champions were fed figs. They contain more mineral matter and are more alkaline than most fruits, are great producers of energy and vitality. They are an excellent natural laxative for sluggish bowels. The high mucin content and tiny seeds help gather and eliminate toxic waste and mucous in the colon. Figs also help kill pernicious bacteria while promoting beneficial friendly lactobacillus acidophilus bacteria in the bowel. It is one of the highest assimilable sources of calcium in the plant kingdom.

***Flax Seed:** Flaxseed is a decongestant, expectorant, laxative, and purgative. Flaxseed alleviates problems of constipation, distension, and discomfort in the abdominal region. They are energizing and help relieve asthma and chronic cough, enrich the blood and strengthen the nerves. Also good for brittle hair. One of the best vegetarian sources of Omega 3 fatty acids. It reduces serum triglyceride levels in patients with heart conditions. It contains up to 60% LNA (linolenic acid), which inhibits the production of tumor-promoting acid in the body and helps maintain the integrity of cell walls along with eight essential amino acids and lecithin. Ancient Indian scriptures state that to reach the highest state of contentment and joy, flax seeds should be eaten daily.

***Cilantro:** Cilantro is antispasmodic, diuretic, and aids in digestion. Cilantro helps to purify the blood and strengthen the heart. Also useful for gas, nausea, and vomiting.

***Ginger:** Antispasmodic, appetizer, astringent, and a diaphoretic (increase perspiration, usually through dilation of capillaries near the surface of the skin). Ginger promotes general and specific health. Ginger is also a diuretic, expectorant, and stimulant. This is one of the oldest and most popular medicinal spices. It promotes the overall circulation of energy in the body and acts as a stimulant for debilitated, lethargic, or convalescing from sickness. It promotes heat, neutralizes toxins, and aids in digestion and assimilation of food and affecting a systematic cleansing through the skin, bowels, and kidneys. Ginger helps prevent motion sickness and vertigo. It is also gentle enough to use during pregnancy to help ease morning sickness or alleviate colds. Chew the peeled root to stimulate the flow of saliva and soothe a sore throat.

***Honey:** Honey is an antiseptic and laxative. Because it contains potassium and formic acid, honey has the characteristic of being an antiseptic. It is hygroscopic, meaning that honey draws every bit of moisture out of germs, thus killing them. It is universally applied to dress external wounds to keep them sterile and also hastens the healing process. Honey creates heat in the body and is good for healing internal and external ulcers. It acts as a carrier for the medicinal properties of herbs for bodily tissues. It is an excellent blood purifier and is good for the eyes and teeth. It is recommended to get quality organic raw honey from producers that do not feed the bees antibiotics, sugar syrup, sulfur drugs, or whose honey contains pesticides and other toxic residues. Darker honey is richer in minerals as compared to light honey.

***Juniper berries:** Juniper berries are antiseptic and carminative (an agent that checks the formation of gas in the gastrointestinal tract and aids in dispelling whatever gas has already formed). Juniper berries are also a diuretic, stimulant, and atonic. They contain an aromatic, rich essential oil similar to turpentine oil. Juniper berries gently stimulate the appetite, increasing the production of hydrochloric acid necessary for protein digestion. They counteract flatulence and help remedy gastrointestinal infections, inflammations, and cramps. They also help with kidney infections.

***Kale:** This is a valuable internal body cleanser. If the body is overly acidic, it can generate flatulence. It is beneficial for the digestive and nervous systems, builds up the body's calcium content, and is one of the cancers preventing foods. It is an antioxidant and protects against breast and colon cancer. Kale contains sulfur, which has antibiotic and anti-viral properties. It also stimulates the liver and other tissues.

***Carrots:** Carrots are a diuretic, stimulant, detoxifier that is alkalinizing, cleansing, nourishing, and stimulating to almost every body system. Carrots supply an abundance of assimilable vitamins, minerals, and enzymes to cells, giving them the fuel they require to slough off morbid wastes and rebuild healthy cells. They are one of the best foods for the liver and digestive tract. Carrots help kidney function and help prevent and treat cancers, balance the endocrine system, depress cholesterol levels in the blood, and increase bulk elimination from the colon. They are very rich in the antioxidant beta carotene, the precursor to vitamin A that makes them so beneficial to the eyes and vision. They contain large amounts of silicon, which strengthens the connective tissues and aids in calcium metabolism. They contain an essential oil that kills parasites and unhealthy intestinal bacteria. Potassium salts in carrots account for the diuretic action and help with stomach and intestinal problems.

***Lentils:** Lentils are a straightforward food to digest. They neutralize muscle acids, help build the glands of the body and blood, and provide a rich supply of minerals for nearly every organ, gland, and tissue in the body. Lentils are especially good for the heart and for stomach ulcers and colitis. They must be sprouted to eat.

***Curry:** Curry promotes perspiration, which acts as a natural air conditioner to cool the body as the moisture evaporates on the skin. It also helps to clear the head and nose during a head cold.

***Onion:** Antiseptic, antispasmodic, diuretic, expectorant, stimulant, antihelminthic (an agent that tends to kill and expel intestinal parasitic worms). Plants containing substances that are obnoxious to the worms or act as cathartics have been used for this purpose. Will soothe the pain of a toothache or stifle a cough. An infection fighter and antibiotic, a diuretic, blood pressure regulator, heart tonic (reduces heart rate), contraceptive and aphrodisiac.

They are used for asthma as onions inhibit the production of compounds that cause the bronchial muscles to spasm, thus relaxing the musculature. They are a rich source of the potent anti-cancer bioflavonoid quercetin. The sulfur compounds in onions help to end putrefactive and fermentation processes in the GI tract and help remove heavy metals while also retarding the retention of fluids and cleansing the system of urea (a waste product of nitrogen found in protein). Chewing raw onions for five minutes kills all the germs in your mouth, making it sterile. It could be beneficial the next time you get a cold. According to researchers in the United States and India, onions also kill germs that cause tooth decay.

***Mango:** Mango is beneficial for the kidneys, combats acidity and poor digestion, and is a wonderful disinfectant in the body. It relieves clogged skin pores, reduces cysts, and is a blood cleanser. The juice will help reduce excess body heat as well as fevers.

***Blueberry:** Blueberries are used as a laxative blood cleanser and help improve sluggish circulation. They can also benefit the eyesight (especially night vision). During World War II, British Royal Air Force pilots consumed blueberries before their night missions to improve their ability to see at night. After the war, numerous studies demonstrated that blueberries do, in fact, improve night vision acuity and lead to a quicker adjustment to darkness and faster restoration of visual acuity after exposure to glare. Blueberries protect against the development of cataracts and glaucoma and are quite therapeutic in the treatment of varicose veins, hemorrhoids, and peptic ulcers. They can heal any infection of the mouth, rejuvenate the pancreas, and relieve dysentery. Blueberries are one of the highest sources of iron.

***Peach:** Peaches are diuretic, expectorant, laxative, and sedative. They are easily digested, have a strong alkaline reaction in the body, stimulate the secretion of digestive juices, help improve the skin, and add color to the complexion. They cleanse the system whenever there is kidney and bladder trouble. For a "peaches and cream complexion," apply a poultice of blended fresh peach on the face, let dry, rinse, and pat dry. They also help to destroy worms.

***Strawberry:** Strawberries are highly rated as a skin cleanser food even though skin eruptions may increase at first as they rid the blood of harmful toxins. A cut strawberry rubbed over the face after washing will whiten the skin and remove slight sunburns. Essential for cardiac health, they offer good nutritional energy that is easy to digest and process. All berries, but especially strawberries, are a good source of anti-cancer ellagic acid. Thus, they are among the highest organic sodium fruits and are eliminative and good for the intestinal tract. However, the seeds can be irritating where there is colitis or some other inflammation of the bowel. Considerable vitamin properties are lost during cooking, and although strawberry jelly, jams, and preservatives may taste good, they have only a fraction, if any, of their original natural vitamins. The addition of sugar renders them acidic and, therefore, detrimental to the body.

***Watermelon:** Watermelon is wonderful cooling food in hot weather, good for the treatment of thirst, and relieves mental depression. They contain a whopping 92% water. Watermelon is excellent for dieters. It is a perfect cleanser and detoxifier for the whole body and has the greatest dissolving power of inorganic minerals in the body out of all the fruits and vegetables. Surprisingly, it has only half the sugar of an apple but tastes much sweeter because sugar is its main producing element. One of nature's safest and most dependable diuretics, watermelon has a remarkable ability to wash out the bladder quickly and completely. The white rind of the watermelon is one of the highest organic sodium foods in nature, and the outside peel is one of the best sources of chlorophyll. Juice the rind along with the red flesh, and drink.

***Olives and olive oil:** Asia Minor is credited as the original home of one of the oldest fruit trees known to humanity, the olive tree. Cultivated in the Near East and eastern Mediterranean regions since the Neolithic Age, records show that this evergreen tree was being cultivated as one of the chief staples of husbandry (breeding of crops) and trade since the early days of old Minoan Crete (3000 BC). Olive oil is easily digested and imparts a generally soothing and healing influence on the digestive tract. Therapeutically, olive oil is beneficial to the gall bladder and liver, strengthens and develops body tissues, and is a general tonic for the nerves.

Taken internally, it increases the secretion of bile and acts as a laxative by encouraging muscular contraction in the bowels. Mild in its action, olive oil can be given to children where more potent laxatives might be harmful. It is also soothing to the mucous membranes and helps dissolve cholesterol deposits.

Essentially, the oil is good for sunburn and other burns and dry skin, minor eruptions, and inflammation. Olive oil is rich in vitamins that nourish the skin's epidermis layer. A lotion made of olive oil and a squeeze of lemon juice will quickly undo the damage done by heavy labor or too much scrubbing. A mixture of olive oil and lime water is recommended for burns. Organic olives are a delicious and nutritious treat that brings many health benefits to the body.

They are full of protein and good fats that help the body release bad fats, and they make the skin beautiful and the hair shiny. They are extremely high in calcium but also contain magnesium, phosphorous, potassium, zinc, copper, manganese, beta carotene, thiamine, riboflavin, niacin pyridoxine, folic acid, and ascorbic acid, bringing youth and vitality to the body. Include some raw organic olives in your diet, and you will see the benefits right before your eyes.

***Oranges:** Oranges are carminative (they relieve flatulence), a stimulant, and a tonic. They aid in toning up and purifying the entire system, acting as an internal antiseptic, tonic stimulant, and a supportive agent. Oranges aid in digestion by stimulating the activity of the glands in the stomach. They are rich in lime and alkaline salts that counteract the tendency towards acidosis. They also have a gentle stimulating effect on the colon. Orange juice does not require any enzymes for digestion.

***Celery:** Celery is an excellent diuretic. Celery contains compounds known as coumarins that are useful in cancer prevention, enhancing the activity of certain white blood cells. These compounds also tone the vascular system, lower blood pressure, and be useful in migraines. It is a favorite reducing food due to its low caloric content. Strongly alkaline, celery counteracts acidosis, halts digestive fermentation of foods, purifies the bloodstream, aids in digestion, and can help clear up skin conditions. If there is stiffness, creaking, or cracking in the joints, our bodies lack organic sodium (the "youth" element that helps keep our body limber and pliable) and have built up inorganic calcium deposits. Celery's rich organic content dislodges these calcium deposits from joints and holds them in solution to be excreted by the kidneys. It also provides organic calcium and silicon for the repair of damaged ligaments and bones.

***Oregano:** Oregano helps to rid the body of poisons, strengthens the stomach, and expels gas from the gastrointestinal tract. It stimulates the liver to increase bile production, which helps emulsify fats in the duodenum and increase peristalsis. It also has anti-fungal, anti-viral, and antibiotic properties.

***Pineapple:** Pineapple is a detoxicant and a diuretic. The pineapple became an important medicinal plant early on. Its fermented juice was made into an alcoholic drink used for fevers and to relieve body heat. Externally, pineapple juice was made for dissolving painful corns and to cure skin ailments. Pineapple contains a fair amount of acid, notably citric, malic, and tartaric acids, which, in their organic form, act as a diuretic, aid in digestion and elimination, and help clear mucous waste from bronchial tissues. They are very rich in bromelain, a proteolytic (protein digesting) enzyme. Bromelain digests dead or diseased cells and foreign microbes in the throat. The most significant value of pineapple juice lies in its digestive power, closely resembling that of human gastric juice.

***Sea vegetables:** The use of seaweed and sea vegetables as food and medicine is not new. The medicinal properties of these highly versatile foods are voluminous. Human blood contains all 100 or so minerals and trace elements found in the ocean. Seaweeds contain up to 10-20 times the value of these elements compared to land plants. In the most assimilable form, because their minerals and elements are integrated into living plant tissue, they are excellent food and medicine. The benefits include reducing blood cholesterol and helping disorders of the Genito-urinary and reproductive systems. Sea vegetables have antibiotic properties known to be effective against penicillin-resistant bacteria and are credited with anti-aging properties. They also hold considerable water when passing through the digestive tract, forming a gel that increases the bulk and transit time for elimination. The Chinese use kelp and other seaweeds to soften and reduce hardened masses in the body. They contain a full range of minerals, including trace minerals, so often deficient in people with degenerative diseases.

Studies conducted at Canada's McGill University have shown that some seaweeds, including arame, hijiki, and kombu, can help remove radioactive strontium in the blood and carry it out of the body. Seaweeds are a few good sources of organic fluorine, a nutrient that boosts the body's defenses and strengthens the teeth and bones. Since fluorine is lost with even minimal cooking, one must eat dried seaweeds (after soaking) to gain any fluorine benefit. The iodine content in seaweed prevents goiters and is indispensable to thyroid function. The thyroid influences digestive and metabolic efficiency, and an iodine deficiency can result in a lack of energy and an inability to metabolize food, not to mention weight gain. Sea vegetables have long been acclaimed as beauty aids and are believed to help maintain beautiful skin and lustrous hair.

***Sprouts:** Reduce inflammation, obtain a laxative effect, aid in remedying rheumatism, and building and tonifying the body. The life energy and enzymes in fresh sprouts stimulate the body's inherent self-cleansing and self-healing ability. If heavy cooked foods are avoided, the overall metabolism is speeded up because it is not weighed down by hard-to-digest food. Their high-water content helps flush poisons from the system, thus slowing the aging clock. They can also destroy cancer cells. They enhance sex life, producing more and better vitamin E.

***Sunflower Seeds:** Sunflower seeds act as a diuretic and an expectorant. They nourish the entire body by supplying it with many vital elements needed for growth and repair. They are a rich source of protein of high biological value, being richer than meats, eggs, and cheese (with no putrefying bacteria). As a good source of vitamin D, sunflower seeds are superior to cod liver oil, which has many objectionable features. In addition to vitamin D, these seeds are richer in the B complex vitamins than an equivalent amount of wheat germ and contain vitamins E and K. Fresh sunflower seeds contain pectin, which binds radioactive residue removes them from the body. These seeds have also been found to relieve farsightedness, eyestrain, and extreme sensitivity to light. They also strengthen brittle fingernails.

***Tahini:** Tahini is made from sesame seeds, which serve as an emollient and a laxative. They help relieve local swelling, and their high vitamin E content strengthens the nerves and heart. Sesamin, a lignan that exists exclusively and abundantly in sesame seeds, has demonstrated remarkable antioxidant effects and has been put to good use in stabilizing sesame products. It inhibits the absorption of cholesterol from the diet and inhibits the manufacture of cholesterol in the liver.

***Zucchini:** Zucchini is highly alkaline and is an excellent remedy for acidosis of the liver and blood. It is nutritionally packed and one of the mildest and easiest vegetables to digest. It is low in calories and exceptionally high in vitamin A and potassium. Zucchini also reduces inflammation and expels roundworms and tapeworms.

***Basil:** Basil acts as an antiseptic, antispasmodic, appetizer, carminative, and warming and moistening herb. It has a good affinity with the stomach, stimulating the appetite, digestion, and nerves. It counteracts flatulence, stomach cramps, nausea, vomiting, and constipation. Tea made from the leaves is recommended for nausea, gas pains, and dysentery.

Smoothies:

Smoothies can be very beneficial to one's health. They can even be used as a meal replacement when the proper ingredients are combined. I have been using a Vitamix juicer for decades because, unlike many traditional juice extractors which discard the fiber so important for digestion, this machine has the unique ability to retain all the important fiber due to its unique design. There might be other comparable units on the market, but, as I said, I have been using this particular unit for decades and am quite satisfied with its performance.

Here are some of the many potential benefits of including smoothies in the diet:

- Upregulates assimilation of nutrients.
- Enhances digestion.
- Improves energy.
- Strengthens bone structure.
- Upregulates the Immune system.
- Lowers cholesterol levels in the blood.
- Enhances gut transit time due to high fiber content.
- Weight loss

If one is somewhat knowledgeable on this subject, there is no limit to the beneficial combination of foods created with smoothies. However, I would like to share some of my favorites that I demonstrated with patients during classes at Naturalife Wellness Center in Long Island, New York, and students at the Living Food Institute in Atlanta, Georgia, where I was a Certified Educator, and learned about these wonderful smoothies from Brenda Cobb, the Institute founder.

Note: Always use organic ingredients and filtered water.

Brenda's Super-Charge Smoothie

1 cup kale
1 cup spinach
1 apple or fresh cup of pineapple (N.B. peel and remove seeds of apple, which contain arsenic)
¼ sprouted mung beans
2 Tbs. Wakame seaweed
½ avocado
2 stalks of celery
1 carrot
½ Tsp. dried mint or 3 Tbs. of fresh mint
1.5 cups water that Wakame seaweed was soaked in

Lemon Basil Energy Smoothie

1 apple
1 cup of sprouted mung beans
2 cups of sprouted sunflower seeds
1 Tsp. kelp seaweed
½ avocado
4 cups of mixed baby greens
1 Tbs. fresh lemon juice
pinch of cayenne pepper
3 Tbs. of fresh basil or 1 Tbs. dried basil
2-4 cups of filtered water
Note: Blend all ingredients until creamy.

Berry Sprout Shake

1 cup strawberries
1 cup blueberries
1 cup raspberries
1 cup broccoli sprouts

2 Tbs. raw coconut oil
1 cup filtered water
Note: Blend for a few seconds until creamy.

Blueberry Blissfulness
2 cups blueberries
2 ripe bananas
1 cup sunflower sprouts
1½ cups filtered water
Note: Blend for a few seconds until creamy.

Strawberry Sunshine
2 cups strawberries
1 ripe banana
1 cup buckwheat sprouts
1 Tbs. raw coconut oil
2 pitted dates (soak in 1 cup of filtered water for 2 hours)

Coconut Avocado Smoothie
Blend the flesh of one young coconut; add one avocado, and blend until creamy and smooth. You may add a vanilla bean or other extracts to create a vanilla shake. Add 2 drops of orange essential oil to create Orange Dream.

Lemon Basil Spice Smoothie
1 deseeded apple
1 handful of sunflower sprouts
1 Tsp. of powdered kelp
½ avocado
2-3 cups of assorted baby greens
juice of 1 lemon
pinch or 2 of cayenne pepper
2 Tbs. of fresh basil
3-4 cups water
Note: Blend until creamy.

Clean Cleanse Smoothie

1 cucumber
3-4 celery stalks
1 cup parsley
1 peeled apple

Detox Smoothie
2 celery stalks
3 large kale leaves
1 cucumber
1 bunch of parsley
1 handful of sprouted sunflower greens
1 handful of buckwheat sprout greens
1 tsp. cayenne pepper
1 large clove of garlic
1 ½ cups purified water
Note: Blend until smooth. Drink this mixture for 3 days. This smoothie will pull toxins from the cells, which may cause detox symptoms of headaches, achy joints, and tiredness. If desired, one can reduce chances of these symptoms by taking an enema.

Supercharge Smoothie
2 apples
1 avocado
2 pitted dates
1 tsp fresh ginger
1½ cups of filtered water
Note: Blend until creamy.

Lively Light Smoothie
1 cup tomato
1 cup celery
1 cup carrot
1 cup cucumber
1 cup red pepper
1 tsp. oregano
1 tsp. cilantro
½ tsp. cayenne pepper

Note: Blend until creamy.

Tropical Bliss
1 cup pitted dates (soak overnight and drain)
1 cup dried mango (soak overnight and drain)
1 cup sliced banana
1 cup dried coconut
1 tsp. vanilla
1 cup whole almonds (soaked overnight and drained)

Banana Sunshine
2 ripe bananas
½ cup strawberries
1 cup sprouts
1 Tbs. raw coconut oil
Note: Blend and add a little water until desired thickness is reached.

Banana Coconut Smoothie
2 ripe bananas
2 Tbs. raw coconut oil
½ tsp. vanilla
¼ cup grated coconut
Filtered water

Green Pineapple Smoothie
1 ripe pineapple
1 bunch green chard
pinch of cayenne pepper
4-5 cups of filtered water

Dr. C's Anti-Inflammatory Smoothie
1 cup of nonacidic fruit (strawberries, blueberries, blackberries)
1 ripe banana sliced and frozen
¼ tsp. black pepper (very important to assimilate the turmeric)
½ tbsp. grated ginger
1/2tbs. Cinnamon

½ tsp. ground turmeric
1 tbsp. fresh-squeezed organic lemon juice
½ cup of organic carrot juice
200 mg. of Magnesium Threonate powder
1 cup of original Silk Almond Milk (DO NOT USE DIAMOND BRAND—IT CONTAINS THE ADDITIVE CARRAGEENAN WHICH IS PRO-INFLAMMATORY)

Healing Folk Remedies:

Source: Wilen, J. Wilen, L., *Bottom Line Healing Remedies*. 2006.

This section includes some classic Folk Medicine remedies for some common minor ailments that have been passed down from one generation to another because they definitely have yielded some positive results in most cases. If you fail to get some slight relief from these time-tested remedies after a few days of usage. I strongly suggest seeking professional care, preferably from a doctor specializing in integrative medicine.

Symptoms tend to overlap each other. In other words, you can have a pain in your side that can be something innocuous like gas or something very serious like appendicitis. Therefore, discontinue the remedy if symptoms persist after a day of usage and seek professional help to be safe. If you get a "clean bill of health," continue the remedy if symptomatic until symptoms abate.

Arthritis

Cherries are said to be effective because they seem to help prevent crystallization of Uric Acid as well as reducing the levels of this acid in the blood. Drinking cherry juice is also effective. Some sources recommend eating cherries and drinking the juice for four days, then stop for four days, then start all over again. Note, eating an excess of cherries can cause diarrhea in some individuals. Also, nightshade vegetables can aggravate arthritic pain in individuals sensitive to this food group (green peppers, tomatoes, white potatoes, and eggplants are the most common). A doctor can perform some tests to determine if someone is sensitive to this food group.

High Cholesterol Remedies

Eating two large apples daily may lower cholesterol levels significantly. Being rich in pectin and bioflavonoids, they can form a gel in the stomach that keeps fats in food from being totally absorbed.

Eating half an avocado daily may also have a positive effect on lowering cholesterol. It is high in fat, but it is a monounsaturated fat that is healthy.

Eating a couple of raw carrots has also shown up to an 11% reduction in cholesterol in some individuals. Omega-3 fatty acids can lower fat deposits on the lining of blood vessels. Monounsaturated fatty acid, found in olive oil, is more effective in reducing artery-clogging cholesterol levels than polyunsaturated fats, such as corn oil and sunflower oil (high in Omega-6 fatty acids, which can be pro-inflammatory).

A brief word on eating grapefruit: studies have shown that eating one grapefruit a day for a month can lower LDL (bad cholesterol) by up to 20%. Eating grapefruit can be contra-indicated when taken with certain drugs, especially drugs taken to lower cholesterol (statins), treat allergies, high blood pressure, or erectile dysfunction, or medicines to reduce anxiety, like Xanax, to just name a few. In fact, to date, there are 83 drugs now and climbing, according to research, that has serious drug interaction with grapefruit that could even be fatal. Check with your physician first to see if you should avoid this fruit if on any medication. Quite honestly, this is one fruit I would avoid completely if taking any medication. Although it has many other health benefits and those previously mentioned, I repeat, *it is better to avoid it if taking any medication.*

Bruises

Make a salve by mashing parsley into a teaspoon of butter. Peel a banana and apply the inside of the banana peel to the bruise with a bandage. It will lessen the pain, reduce the discoloration, and speed the healing.

Burns

First Degree Burns: First, apply cold water or a cold compress. Then apply a slice of unpeeled raw potato or a slice of raw onion. Leave on for 15 minutes. Also, puncture a vitamin E capsule and apply it directly to the burn. Apple cider vinegar (ACV) may also help when poured on the scalded area (only use an acidic solution like ACV on very superficial, minor burns). Aloe Vera is also very good, especially if taken directly from an aged plant at least a few years old. It's a good idea to keep this plant in the home for that very reason. Honey is also good for pain from the burn.

Second-Degree Burns: Submerge the burned area in cold water for 30 mins. DO NOT USE BUTTER, LARD, OR A SALVE ON THIS BURN! They are a breeding ground for bacteria. If the burn is on the arm or leg, keep the limb elevated to prevent swelling.

Severe Burns, Third-Degree Burns, Chemical or Acid Burns: SEEK MEDICAL ATTENTION IMMEDIATELY! For chemical or acid burns, subject the area to running water to wash away chemicals until help arrives.

Colds and Flu

Chicken soup has been used for centuries for these types of respiratory symptoms. Controlled studies have been performed using broncho fiberscopes and measurements of mucous velocity, which proved the efficacy of taking this age-old remedy. I made garlic chicken soup whenever anyone in my family came down with a cold or flu, which led to the condition running its course much quicker. There are many variations from which you can choose. The trick is to be very generous when adding garlic to the soup.

Sore Throat

In a cup of filtered water, simmer ½ cup of raisins for 20 minutes and drink (you can also eat the raisins if you'd like.) (Tibetan remedy).

Add 2 tsp. of apple cider vinegar to a cup of warm filtered water. Gargle a mouthful and spit out, then swallow a mouthful. Keep this up until the liquid is all gone.

Warm 1/2 cup of Kosher Salt in a frying pan. Pour the salt into a large white handkerchief and fold so that none of the salt can ooze out. Wrap the hanky around the neck for one hour.

Constipation

½ cup of lemons, stewed prunes, 2 peeled apples, or a half-dozen dried figs. Soak them overnight in 1 cup of warm filtered water. Then you can drink the water and eat the figs.

Flax Seeds: 1-2 Tbs. with lots of water right after lunch or dinner.

Eat a Tbs. of raisins that have been soaking for a few hours before the main meal.

Cough

Squeeze the juice of one lemon into a glass. Add hot water, 2 Tbs. of honey, and a half stick of cinnamon. (Diabetics should avoid honey.)

Mash cooked oats with honey and eat when the coughing spell starts.

1 cup of Licorice tea. Licorice root contains saponins, natural substances known to break up and loosen mucous.

Note: Licorice is contraindicated for those with high blood pressure or kidney problems.

Earache

Fill the ear with three drops of warm olive oil and plug the ear with a cotton ball. Repeat 3-4 times a day until the earache is gone.

Mix the juice from a grated fresh ginger with an equal amount of sesame oil. Put 3 drops of this mixture in the ear canal and plug the ear with a cotton ball. Keep it in for a few hours. You could keep it in the ear for a few hours.

If the earache persists, consult a physician to avoid any serious complications.

Headaches

Research claims that almonds contain salicylates, the pain-relieving ingredient found in aspirin. Eating about 15 almonds should do the work of one aspirin. Granted, it may take a little longer for the headache to vanish, but you will not run the risk of side effects of aspirin (i.e., GI (gastrointestinal) ulcers)

The essence of Rosemary: rub a small amount of oil on the forehead, temples, and behind the ears. In addition, you are inhaling the fumes from the open bottle 3-4 times. If the headache is still present within half an hour, repeat the process.

Note: In rare cases, a headache heralds a serious medical problem, such as meningitis, brain hemorrhage, stroke, or a benign or malignant tumor. Here are Red Flags that would indicate seeking a physician:

- The first headache in your life.
- A headache that worsens over several weeks.
- A change in severity or frequency.

Seek emergency care in these conditions:

- The worst headache to which you have ever been subjected.
- Headache with a stiff neck, vomiting, or fever.
- Signs of abnormal neurological symptoms include double vision, trouble speaking, weakness, or numbness unless suffered before as part of a migraine syndrome.

Indigestion

Hyperacidity – chew a tsp. of some dry rolled oats thoroughly, then swallow. The oats will soothe and neutralize the acid condition.

1 cup of sage tea is also a viable alternative.

1 Tbs. of honey and 2 tsp. of apple cider vinegar mixed in hot water and drink. This remedy is contraindicated for diabetics.

Eating one large radish may also relieve all the symptoms related to indigestion.

1 cup of chamomile or peppermint tea. Either is very soothing if taken at the first sign of indigestion.

Sinus Problems

Slowly and cautiously, gently inhale vapors of freshly grated horseradish mixed with equal amounts of lemon juice.

Crush one clove of garlic into a half-cup of water. Draw the solution into an eyedropper, careful not to include any small pieces of garlic, and insert garlic water into both nostrils. Usually, 10 drops per nostril, 3 times per day for 3 days, should do the trick.

Halitosis (Bad Breath)

Suck on a piece of Cinnamon stick to sweeten the breath.

Floss and brush teeth after meals to prevent small food particles from decaying between teeth.

Hypochlorhydria is the lack of production of hydrochloric acid (HCL) in the stomach. This acid, normally produced by the stomach, is necessary to break down protein for digestion. A lack of HCL can cause the undigested protein to putrefy and also cause bad breath. To treat, add 1 tsp. of apple cider vinegar (ACV) into an 8 oz. glass of water and sip every few bites. ACV contains acetic acid, which will function as a mild form of HCL and will aid in eliminating putrefaction of protein.

Please note, as stated earlier in this section, that symptoms tend to overlap each other. Again, I repeat, you may have a pain in the lower gut which could be something minor like gas or possibly something more serious like appendicitis. Therefore, even though these remedies, for the most part, are successful recommendations for some simple common ailments, it behooves the reader to consult a physician if symptoms persist after trying these remedies.

If the spirit moves you, buy the book *Folk Remedies for Common Ailments*, written by Anne McIntyre. It contains foods, spices, herbs, and essential oils that can treat common ailments. Most of these items are staples found either in your kitchen cupboard, bathroom, or garden if you happen to have a green thumb. The book's back is a chart called "Remedies and Ailments," with suggestions for using specific foods, spices, herbs, and essential oils for specific conditions. For example, chamomile, cinnamon, and parsley provide effective relief for abdominal pains, while garlic, olive oil, oats, and peppermint are good for earaches. In all, there is a combination of over 50 different remedies that, in many cases, can be applied to many different ailments. (The "Remedies and Ailments" chart shows over 40 conditions where several of these remedies may apply.)

Words of Encouragement

Hopefully, you have found the information presented here to be informative and worthwhile. I promise that your potential health benefits can be quite gratifying if you apply these concepts in your life. The decision to apply them is entirely up to you. At this juncture, I believe it is very apropos to tell you one last story to emphasize this point.

The Wise Man

Once upon a time, there lived a wise man. He would regularly travel the countryside, roaming from town to town to help the people with life's challenges.

Like King Solomon, he possessed great wisdom and common sense, always giving people the helpful advice needed for their particular situation. So, you can imagine, he was admired and held in high esteem by everyone throughout the countryside. Well, almost everyone. You see, this young man believed he was the wisest in the land and felt he was not appreciated for his great wisdom.

Eventually, he came to the conclusion that the only way he would ever be appreciated as truly being the wisest in the land was to devise a riddle that would be impossible for the Wise Man to answer correctly. Consequently, he spent many moons trying to come up with such a riddle.

Finally, he concocted what he believed would be the perfect riddle. He figured he would approach the Wise Man with a tiny bird concealed in his clenched fist. He then thought he would ask the Wise Man what he held in that hand. Now, realizing the Wise Man had the gift of discernment, the young man knew that this sage would certainly know that he was concealing a bird in his cupped hand. Still, the young man thought he could stump the Wise Man. He thought that once the Wise Man correctly guessed that he had a bird in his hand, he would then question if the bird was living or dead.

You see, he deduced that if the Wise Man said that the bird in his clenched hand was living, he would just squeeze the life out of the bird before opening his hand and present a dead bird. He then figured if the Wise Man said the bird was, in fact, dead, he would simply open his fist and let the bird fly away. Understandably, he thought he devised a riddle that was impossible for the Wise Man to answer correctly.

The young man waited patiently for many months for the Wise Man to return to his village. Finally, the Wise Man returned to the young man's town. When the town meeting began, the young man immediately approached the Wise Man while all the villagers were still present. Obviously, he wanted everyone to observe his ingenious riddle that was supposedly going to stump the Wise Man, finally making all the villagers realize he was the wisest in the land. So, he approached the Wise Man with his outstretched clenched fist and exclaimed, "Oh, Wise Man, pray tell: what be it I possess in my hand?" The Wise Man stared into the young man's eyes for a moment, then answered, "You have a bird in your hand, My Son!" "That is correct, oh wise one! But tell me, please, be this bird living or dead?" Once again, the Wise Man stared into the young man's eyes for a brief moment and said, "My Son, the answer to that question lies in your own hands!"

You see, my friend, so it is with you. Whether you decide to incorporate any of these concepts into your lifestyle is in your hands.

Since this work was prefaced with a poem I wrote concerning healing, I felt it apropos to conclude with another poem. The theme of this poem, however, focuses on taking the next step and, perhaps, motivate you to "go the extra mile" and have the audacity to seek a healthier and, yes, happier lifestyle by taking responsibility for your health and applying some of the concepts described in this work.

“Choices”

Life's choices truly define who you are,
Like taking a trip when driving a car.
Some wrong turns might be made along the way,
Hopefully, corrected by the end of the day.

As long as you persevere and focus on your goal,
Making wrong turns will take no great toll.

For it’s not important how you arrive,
So long as you get there safe and alive.
The same can be said where your health is concerned,
If you apply these concepts, you just learned.

Sure, there will be times you fall short of the mark,
But easily made right like a walk in the park.

Yes, realize, my friend, that poor choices don't last,
Just develop the mantra, "This too shall pass."
For so long as you succeed more than you fail,
you surely will experience life's "holy grail."

Having a healthy life’s journey, you see,
Possessing the passion to *Be all you can Be.*

So, make the right choice, for you know what to do,
Take the road not taken, traveled by so few.

~ Dr. Sebastian Caliendo

Suggested Readings to
Make Your Journey Healthier and Happier:

Dr. David Minkoff
The Search For The Perfect Protein
Glenn Poveromo
Change Your Thinking, Change Your Life
Dr. Henry G. Bieler
Food is Your Best Medicine
Gregg Braden
The Spontaneous Healing of Belief
Rhonda Byrne
The Secret
Dr. Deepak Chopra
The Healing Self
Perfect Health
Quantum Healing
You are the Universe
Dr. Wayne W. Dyer
Change Your Thoughts – Change Your Life... Living the Wisdom of the Tao
The Keys to Higher Awareness
The Power of Intention
The Secrets of the Power of Intention
Secrets of Your Own Healing Power
We Consciousness: 33 Profound Truths for Inner and Outer Peace
Wisdom of the Ages
Dr. David Friedman
Food Sanity
Dr. David R. Hawkins
Power Vs. Force: The Hidden Determinants of Human Behavior
Louise L. Hay

I Can Do It
You Can Heal Your Life
Bruce H. Lipton, PhD
The Biology of Belief...Unleashing the Power of Consciousness, Matter & Miracles
Dr. Maxwell Maltz
Psycho-Cybernetics
Anne McIntyre
Folk Remedies for Common Ailments
Dr. Joseph Mercola
Effortless Healing
Cory Muscara
Stop Missing Your Life
Dr. Mark Stengler
Natural Healing Encyclopedia
Dr. Jade Tate
The Metabolic Renewal Road Map
Colin Tipping
Radical Forgiveness
Eckhart Tolle
The Power of Now
Karol K. Truman
Feelings Buried Alive Never Die
Mark Zocchi
The Zen Book of Life

Made in United States
Orlando, FL
27 November 2024